Voltaire & D'Alembert

INDIANA UNIVERSITY PRESS

BLOOMINGTON   1962

Voltaire & D'Alembert

BY JOHN N. PAPPAS

Indiana University Humanities Series Number 50
Indiana University, Bloomington, Indiana

EDITOR: Edward D. Seeber
ASSISTANT EDITOR: David H. Dickason
ASSISTANT EDITOR: Hubert C. Heffner

The Indiana University Humanities Series was
founded in 1939 for the publication of occasional
papers and monographs by members of the faculty.

FOREWORD

THE FRIENDSHIP between Voltaire and d'Alembert has been mentioned frequently in studies of the eighteenth century, yet there has thus far been no thorough investigation made of their relationship. D'Alembert is generally considered a lukewarm individual who only sporadically and reluctantly engaged in the struggle to further the ideals of the Enlightenment, whereas Voltaire is presumed to have continued relying on his faint-hearted disciple more out of friendship than because of the geometer's services.

This stereotype is due in part to Voltaire himself who, in his correspondence with his disciples in Paris, complained frequently of their lack of zeal. It is due also to an insufficient knowledge of d'Alembert's aims and methods, which has forced historians to rely too heavily on the Voltairian picture. The present study seeks to remedy this imbalance by supplying background material not heretofore considered in the Voltaire-d'Alembert relationship and, as a result, to present a more comprehensive view of the subject.

I express my sincere appreciation to Professors Norman L. Torrey and Henry H. H. Remak for graciously consenting to read the original manuscript and for their valuable suggestions and criticisms; and I add a special word of thanks to Professor Arthur H. Wilson for reading Chapter V of this study and offering his helpful critiques and encouragement. I am grateful also to Professor Edward D. Seeber and the editors of the Indiana University Humanities Series for their careful scrutiny of the final manuscript.

CONTENTS

Frontispiece drawing of Voltaire by Alexander Mueller
Title-page drawing of D'Alembert by Tracy Lahey

*The Encyclopedic
Venture*

O N E *

WHEN Mme du Châtelet died, in November, 1749, Voltaire had already achieved a literary reputation. Despite the unfavorable effect of his *Lettres philosophiques,* published in 1734, on the French authorities, Mme du Châtelet had managed to keep his literary production in the more acceptable fields of literature and science, thus offsetting the suspicions aroused by his earlier philosophical speculation.[1] During this period he had gained favor at court and had been elected to the Académie française through his public profession of a return to orthodoxy. Left rudderless upon the death of Mme du Châtelet, Voltaire for a time continued the society life he had previously been pursuing.

Precisely at this time a young mathematician, Jean Le

* The system of references used in the body of the text is explained in Footnote 2 of this chapter. Direct quotations have been given in modernized French for the convenience of the reader.

1. This is not to say that Voltaire abandoned his unorthodox interests but that, as Ira Wade points out in his *Voltaire and Mme du Châtelet* (Princeton, 1941), pp. 190–92, most of his contemporaries were unaware of this activity, which remained clandestine at the time.

Rond d'Alembert, had begun, through Mme du Deffand's' salon, to make contacts with the literary and social world whose shining light, by then, was Voltaire. If the obscure geometer met the great author of *La Henriade* in such a milieu, the acquaintance must have started with the usual superficial introductions in a salon. Little is known, in fact, of their relations during this period. The earliest record we have of any exchange between them is a letter from Voltaire, dated 13 December 1746, thanking d'Alembert for sending a copy of his *Réflexions sur la cause générale des vents*. He and Mme du Châtelet, Voltaire assures the author, will read it with pleasure, and he adds: "Il n'y a point de maison où vous soyez plus estimé."[2] By 1750 they seem to have been on sufficiently friendly terms for Voltaire to invite him to a private reading of his latest play, *Rome sauvée*. After the performance, d'Alembert is said to have told Voltaire that the line "Permettez que César ne parle point de lui" might better have been omitted. To which the author replied: "Si je n'avais eu que des hommes tels que vous pour spectateurs, je ne l'aurais pas

2. *Voltaire's Correspondence,* ed. Theodore Besterman (Genève, 1953—), XV, 156. Raymond Naves does not seem to be aware of this letter (quoted by Gustave Desnoiresterres, *Voltaire et la société au XVIIIe siècle* [Paris, 1867—76], IV, 395) when he refers to d'Alembert's letter to Voltaire dated 24 August 1762 saying: ". . . on constate qu'avant cette lettre aucune relation n'existait entre eux." *Voltaire et l'Encyclopédie* (Paris, 1938), p. 11. To avoid unnecessary footnotes, all references to the Moland edition of Voltaire's *Œuvres complètes* (Paris, 1877—85) will appear parenthetically in the text with only the volume and page numbers given. Voltaire's correspondence is quoted preferably from the Besterman edition (designated as "Best."), and only those letters not yet published in that series when this study was written are quoted from Moland or other sources. Citations from the Belin edition of d'Alembert's *Œuvres* (Paris, 1821) will be identified as "D'Al." Diderot's *Œuvres,* ed. Assézat-Tourneux (Paris, 1875—79) will be indicated by "AT.," and his *Correspondance,* ed. Georges Roth (Paris, 1955), will be referred to as "Roth."

écrit" (V, 266).[3] Aside from these courteous exchanges, it does not appear that relations between the two men had progressed beyond such mundane contacts. Even these were probably limited, since Voltaire lived in semi-seclusion at Cirey with Mme du Châtelet, and his departure from Paris shortly after her death prevented them from developing further.

The loss of favor with Mme de Pompadour, and the king's coolness toward him, caused Voltaire to withdraw from the social pursuits he had enjoyed while Mme du Châtelet was still alive, and he accepted the pressing invitations of Frederick of Prussia to join his circle of "libres penseurs" in Potsdam. In this atmosphere, safe from the inhibiting influence of the censors, Voltaire pursued with renewed vigor his previously suppressed interests and began to produce a series of irreligious and critical works,[4] which were no doubt greeted with pleasure in France by the growing movement against existing authority. The Philosophes had only recently found organization and expression in the Encyclopédie, whose prospectus in 1751

3. The quotation is from the Kehl edition. The same incident is recorded by Cousin d'Avalon as follows: "Ce vers est de trop, dit d'Alembert. Oui, répondit Voltaire, si tous les spectateurs vous ressemblaient; mais il fallait les avertir de la modestie de César." D'Alembertiana (Paris, 1813), p. 40. D'Alembert was quite frank in his criticisms of his friends' works. When in 1761 he pointed out to Rousseau a number of passages in La Nouvelle Héloïse which might well be deleted, the author replied: "Je suis charmé, Monsieur, de la lettre que vous venez de m'écrire et loin de me plaindre de votre louange, je vous en remercie, parce qu'elle est jointe à une critique franche et judicieuse qui me fait aimer l'une et l'autre comme le langage de l'amitié." Rousseau, Correspondance générale, ed. Dufour (Paris, 1924–34), VI, 26.

4. Some of these works were La Voix du sage et du peuple (1750), Idées de la Mothe Le Vayer (1751), Micromégas (1752), Abrégé de l'histoire universelle (1753). La Pucelle was also circulating in Paris at this time.

had announced that Diderot and d'Alembert were to be the editors of the new enterprise. The name of Diderot, who only two years earlier had been imprisoned for atheistic tendencies in his *Lettre sur les aveugles,* probably caused the authorities some concern, and, in fact, the new publication met with immediate resistance, particularly from the Jesuits in their *Journal de Trévoux.*[5]

When the young abbé de Prades presented at the Sorbonne on 18 November 1751 a thesis echoing the naturalistic principles of Locke as expounded in d'Alembert's "Discours préliminaire" to the *Encyclopédie,* the ensuing controversy must have convinced the detractors of the publication that their earlier fears had been justified; but for many believers, the de Prades affair was the first revelation that a "plot" had been formed against the Christian religion. The Sorbonne approved the thesis without too close a scrutiny only to realize later that it had thereby compromised its own orthodoxy. The thesis was belatedly condemned, de Prades was deprived of his academic standing, and the Encyclopedists were accused of having inspired his irreligious principles. In the following year, Volume II of the *Encyclopédie* appeared containing de Prades's article, "Certitude," which recapitulated his thesis. Thus the link with the Encyclopedists was firmly established, and the *Encyclopédie* was in turn condemned and finally suppressed by the Conseil d'état.[6]

The aims of the *Encyclopédie,* and the difficulties encountered by its editors, were bound to evoke Voltaire's sympathies. Although not connected directly with the pub-

5. See my *Berthier's Journal de Trévoux and the Philosophes* (Vol. III, *Studies on Voltaire and the Eighteenth Century.* Genève, 1957), pp. 163–72.

6. Cf. ibid., pp. 185–86. A detailed account of the de Prades affair and its effect on the *Encyclopédie* may be found in Arthur M. Wilson's *Diderot: the Testing Years* (New York, 1957), pp. 154–60.

lication, he expressed his admiration for this "immense and immortal" work in his *Siècle de Louis XIV* (1751).[7] Praise from so famous a writer was no doubt encouraging to the Encyclopedists, and it was natural that d'Alembert, when seeking asylum for the abbé de Prades, should think of the author of the *Siècle de Louis XIV*. He wrote Voltaire, asking his support in obtaining a post for de Prades with Frederick of Prussia and, to reinforce his request, sought Mme Denis's aid in obtaining her uncle's assent.[8] This added precaution was unnecessary: Voltaire was only too glad to help the ill-fated abbé. D'Alembert promptly wrote Voltaire on 24 August 1752 thanking him for his assistance in placing de Prades at Frederick's court, as well as for the praise of the *Encyclopédie* in Voltaire's history of Louis XIV. The letter, which also announced the renewal of publication of the *Encyclopédie,* can be considered the beginning of a correspondence destined to last until Voltaire's death in 1778.[9]

How Voltaire first became a collaborator on the *Encyclopédie* is not certain. It is generally thought that he did so at d'Alembert's request.[10] It has also been suggested

7. XIV, 153. D'Alembert had inserted high praise for Voltaire in the "Discours préliminaire" of the *Encyclopédie* appearing in July, 1751. Shortly thereafter (December, 1751), he had a further opportunity to show his appreciation of Voltaire's praise when Crébillon refused to give his approbation for the latter's *Mahomet.* "On chercha donc un autre censeur à la tragédie," Gustave Desnoiresterres tells us, "et le choix se porta sur d'Alembert, dont l'approbation, cela va de source, ne se fit pas attendre." *Voltaire et la société,* IV, 188.

8. Ibid., p. 395.

9. XXI, 37–38. The earlier relations between the two were the impersonal, mundane contacts usually made in salon society and do not seem to have engendered any close or lasting ties.

10. See for example René Pomeau, *La Religion de Voltaire* (Paris, 1956), p. 286; and Ira Wade, "The Search for a New Voltaire," *Transactions of the American Philosophical Society,* Vol. XLVIII (1958), Part 4, p. 83.

that as early as 1752, Voltaire was interested in becoming an Encyclopedist but that Frederick opposed this desire.[11] Some evidence for the thesis that Voltaire took the initiative can be deduced from a letter to d'Alembert, dated 20 May 1754, in which Voltaire writes from Colmar: "A propos d'âme, j'avais pris la liberté d'envoyer à une certaine personne un petit mot sur l' 'âme,' non pas pour qu'on en fît usage, mais seulement pour montrer que je m'étais intéressé à l'*Encyclopédie*" (Best., XXIV, 262). A letter from Frederick late in 1752 suggests that the article "Âme" had been written by Voltaire for his own projected *Dictionnaire philosophique* because the monarch refers to "votre dictionnaire" and "l'ouvrage que vous faites" (Best., XXI, 116-17). Had Voltaire later sent the same article to the *Encyclopédie* for consideration? Or is the "certaine personne" mentioned to d'Alembert simply Frederick, as Besterman seems to intimate? (Best., XXIV, 263, n. 11). The same letter to d'Alembert, sending "stones" to "stuff into a few corners of the wall," indicates that Voltaire is sending them at the request of the Encyclopedist: "J'ai obéi comme j'ai pu à vos ordres" (Best., XXIV, 262). Unless the missing letters from d'Alembert to Voltaire are discovered, the question must remain unresolved.

What concerns us here is that, in his further relations with the *Encyclopédie*, Voltaire was drawn closer to d'Alembert, with whom he corresponded, and whom he considered the most important man in the encyclopedic enterprise.[12] Their early correspondence deals almost exclusively with the *Encyclopédie*. Voltaire promptly sends the

11. A more detailed treatment of this question can be found in Naves, p. 9.

12. When relating to Grimm her visit to Voltaire in 1757, Mme d'Epinay wrote: "Croiriez-vous qu'on ne parle que de d'Alembert lorsqu'il est question de l'*Encyclopédie?*" XXXIX, 333.

articles requested of him and, along with high praise for the enterprise, he occasionally makes suggestions and criticisms for certain articles in the *Encyclopédie* which do not meet his approval. D'Alembert, for his part, is almost obsequious in his praise and expressions of gratitude, and it is evident that he is anxious to have Voltaire's good will and cooperation. That he succeeded is indicated in the gradual change from the business-like tone of their earlier correspondence to one of mutual admiration and respect. D'Alembert's visit in August, 1756, to Voltaire's home completed the process, and, as René Pomeau puts it, the Encyclopedist "conquit définitivement la confiance du grand homme."[13] That the trust was mutual can be seen by the note of warmth that their subsequent correspondence reveals.

Perhaps one of the most apparent marks of esteem which d'Alembert showed toward Voltaire after visiting him was the article, "Genève," which d'Alembert wrote and inserted, despite Diderot's disapproval,[14] into Volume VII of the *Encyclopédie*. There is no doubt that much of the article was written at Voltaire's request and that d'Alembert was "paying his court" to the master, as Rousseau had phrased it.[15] On 6 December 1757 Voltaire thanks d'Alembert for having supported his position in the *Encyclopédie* (Best., XXXII, 210), and the following month he admits: "On se plaint de l'article des 'Comédiens' inséré dans celui de Genève; mais vous avez joint ce petit mot de

13. *La Religion*, p. 330.
14. See Wilson, *Diderot*, pp. 282–83, for Diderot's attitude toward the article.
15. *Correspondance générale*, ed. Dufour, IV, 17. Later Rousseau again wrote to Vernet: "Je n'ignorais pas que l'article *Genève* était en partie de M. de Voltaire; quoique j'aie eu la discretion de n'en rien dire, il vous sera aisé de voir par la lecture de l'ouvrage que je savais en l'écrivant à quoi m'en tenir." Ibid., p. 91.

la comédie à la requête des citoyens qui vous en ont prié"
(Best., XXXIII, 85).

Rousseau's *Lettre à M. d'Alembert sur les spectacles*
was the least of the difficulties engendered by "Genève."
D'Alembert's praise of the Genevan ministers for their
"perfect Socinianism" aroused a storm against the *Encyclopédie* not only from the French authorities, who saw
in this praise an implied criticism of their own religion,
but from the Genevan pastors as well, since the compro-
mising praise was tantamount to an accusation that they had
abandoned Christianity for a sort of Deism.[16] The situation was aggravated for the Encyclopedists by the attempted assassination of Louis XV that same year (1757),
because their republican doctrines were thought to have
undermined legitimate authority and encouraged sedition.
D'Alembert, who preferred his tranquility to harassment
by the censors, resigned from the enterprise. On 11 January 1758 he explained his decision to Voltaire,[17] and the
latter, in a letter dated 19 January, pleaded with him to
remain on the editorial staff of the *Encyclopédie* (Best.,
XXXIII, 60). He even wrote to Diderot, asking him to
dissuade his co-editor from his resolution. Without waiting
for his reply to his first letter, d'Alembert again wrote his

16. A full account of the difficulties experienced as a result of
d'Alembert's article is given in Wilson, *Diderot*, pp. 275–90.

17. Best., XXXIII, 35. Naves, p. 54, calls this letter a "refus cas-
sant" of Voltaire's plea not to abandon the *Encyclopédie*. Since the
only previous letter by Voltaire to d'Alembert mentioning the latter's
defection is that of 8 January, it is more probable that d'Alembert
would not have received the letter from Switzerland in just three days
and that their letters crossed. D'Alembert's letter of 11 January would
therefore not be a rejection of Voltaire's plea but simply a statement
of intention. Naves suggests that Voltaire ignored d'Alembert's reasons
in the letter of 11 January and did not change his mind until d'Alembert's second letter (20 January) on the subject.

friend on 20 January reiterating the futility of publishing
a work which was to be still more severely censored than
before and reaffirming his intention to quit (Best.,
XXXIII, 66). But his first letter had already had its effect
on Voltaire. On 29 January he writes d'Alembert admitting that he had been unaware that the attacks against the
Encyclopédie had been authorized. Everyone must leave
the publication, he pursues: ". . . il ne faut point que la
tête se sépare du corps" (Best., XXXIII, 86). Evidently
the news of official approval of the attacks against the
Encyclopédie had persuaded Voltaire to take d'Alembert's
view of the matter,[18] but we should not underestimate
Voltaire's feelings of friendship and loyalty for d'Alembert
as factors that influenced this decision. As has been noted,
at least some of the difficulties experienced by the Encyclopedists at this time had been brought on by "Genève"—
which had been written at the inspiration of Voltaire. In
fact, Voltaire himself assumed a share of the responsibility
for these difficulties. In his letter of 29 January condon-
ing d'Alembert's decision he alludes to the rumor that
d'Alembert is quitting because of the repercussions over his
article and laments: "Plût à dieu que vous n'eussiez point
vu de prêtres quand vous vîntes chez nous!" (Best.,
XXXIII, 86). Since to him d'Alembert was the "head"
of the enterprise, and since he felt somewhat responsible
for his disciple's present difficulties, it would have been
natural for him to uphold d'Alembert's position rather
than that of Diderot, who was comparatively unknown to
him. Yet Voltaire continued his collaboration with the
Encyclopédie, hoping that d'Alembert would return to his
position as co-editor and urging him to do so (Best.,

18. Naves, p. 55, attributes Voltaire's abandonment of the *Encyclopédie* exclusively to his realization that the attacks against it were
officially protected.

XXXIII, 182, 207, 224, 227, 243, 264, 278).[19] Then, when
it became clear that d'Alembert was not going to change
his mind, Voltaire urged all the Encyclopedists to follow
the action of their "leader" in abandoning the publication.
Thereafter Voltaire, although continuing to pursue its
attackers, ceased to contribute directly to the *Encyclopédie*.

Despite his withdrawal, Voltaire had profited from the
experience. It has served to make him more aware of his
raison d'être. The encyclopedic cause had imbued him
with a sense of mission and had opened before him the
vision of his rôle as leader and defender of the Philosophes.
The crystallization of this dream in Voltaire's mind is due
in large measure to d'Alembert. It was he who first elicited
Voltaire's active participation in the movement and who,
through frequent references to the activities of their enemies, aroused Voltaire's indignation and desire to counterattack. Initially, this was done by pointing out the difficulties under which the Encyclopedists were working.
Thus, when Voltaire complained in 1757 that many
articles in the *Encyclopédie* reflected too orthodox an
opinion, d'Alembert had replied: "Sans doute nous avons
de mauvais articles de Théologie et de métaphysique, mais
avec des censeurs Théologiens, et un privilège, je vous
défie de les faire meilleurs" (Best., XXXI, 237). As Voltaire's interest became greater, d'Alembert became more
specific and pointed to the activity of the Jesuits, particularly of Berthier, the editor of their *Journal de Trévoux*,
in the suppression and harassment of the *Encyclopédie*.[20]

19. Voltaire, in a letter to Théodore Tronchin, expresses his conviction that d'Alembert will reconsider: "Je ne crois point du tout que
M. d'Alembert renonce à l'*Encyclopédie*. Il se dégoûte quelquefois,
mais il se rengage aisément. Ce grand ouvrage a besoin de lui. On ne
souffrira pas qu'il l'abandonne." *Lettres inédites aux Tronchin*, ed.
B. Gagnebin (Genève and Lille, 1950), II, 10.

20. Moland XL, 45, 96; Best., XXXI, 26–27, 147–48; XXXIII, 35.
An account of Voltaire's relations with the *Journal de Trévoux* and

When finally, in 1757–58, the intensified campaign against the publication broke out, Voltaire was prepared to devote all his energies to its defense. He wrote to Diderot, for example, encouraging him to stand firm in the face of the attacks and asked for the names of the attackers (XXXIX, 364). D'Alembert's withdrawal from the *Encyclopédie* left Voltaire momentarily undecided as to a course of action, but he soon regained his zeal. On 4 May 1759, he tells d'Alembert that he intends to attack Berthier and "tutti quanti" (XL, 89), to which d'Alembert replies: ". . . mon cher ami, frappez fort; vous êtes en place marchande pour cela" (XL, 96). Several months later d'Alembert reminds Voltaire that the persecutions are continuing (XL, 263), and the latter replies with a copy of his satire *Les Quand.* In thanking Voltaire for this attack on their mutual enemies, d'Alembert writes of the joy of those who, living in "an enslaved and sheeplike nation," have a philosopher in a free country who can raise his voice in their defense (XL, 351). He will return frequently to this idea in his future correspondence. When, in reacting to his announcement of Palissot's *Les Philosophes modernes*, Voltaire complains of the inactivity of the Philosophes in the face of such attacks, d'Alembert reiterates the theme suggested in his previous letter by retorting: "Vous êtes indigné, dites-vous, que les philosophes se laissent égorger; vous en parlez bien à votre aise: et que voulez-vous qu'ils fassent? . . . C'est à vous, mon cher maître, qui êtes à la tête des lettres, . . . c'est à vous, qui n'avez rien à craindre, à venger l'honneur des gens de lettres outragés" (XL, 380).

This statement is significant in exposing d'Alembert's conception of Voltaire's future rôle in the Philosophe cause. Having abandoned the encyclopedic enterprise ex-

---

the Jesuits may be found in my "La Rupture entre Voltaire et les Jésuites," *Lettres Romanes* (Louvain), XIII (1959), 351–70, as well as in the Voltaire chapter of *Berthier's "Journal de Trévoux."*

cept to furnish the articles on mathematics already con-
tracted for, d'Alembert now envisaged a new approach to
the furtherance of "philosophy." Voltaire, and not the
Encyclopédie, would henceforth be the focal point of the
movement. This leadership would entail the shepherd's
defense of his "little flock" in Paris while the latter, in
turn, would seek to strengthen and increase their ranks
by assuming an air of respectability and avoiding open
identification with the "conspiracy" label attached to the
Encyclopedists.[21] It is small wonder that Diderot accused
d'Alembert of being the *Encyclopédie's* determined enemy
and of seeking to destroy it.[22] And it is not surprising that
he had misgivings about Voltaire.[23]

21. Details concerning this movement will be elaborated upon in
a forthcoming study on d'Alembert.

22. Roth, II, 120.

23. Cf. Wilson, *Diderot,* p. 283, and Norman L. Torrey, "Voltaire's
Reaction to Diderot," *PMLA,* L (December, 1935), 1109.

A New Approach

TWO

THE CORRESPONDENCE between Voltaire and d'Alembert from 1760 on reveals a steady delineation by d'Alembert of what is expected by "the flock" from its leader. By now he no doubt felt secure in his influence on Voltaire, who had abandoned the *Encyclopédie* on his account and had complied willingly when, on May 1760, d'Alembert had asked him to withdraw his play *Médime* from the actors who had performed Palissot's *Philosophes* (XL, 397). But more important was the fact that Voltaire was becoming increasingly dependent on him as a major source of information on the progress of "the brothers" and their struggle against "l'Infâme." When, in 1758, the concerted attack against the *Encyclopédie* had reached its peak, Voltaire had felt woefully uninformed of what was happening. For want of any news from Diderot's side, d'Alembert's detailed information had been decisive in causing him to abandon the publication. At that time Voltaire had written his friend concerning its persecution: "Je n'en sais rien; je vois tout de trop loin. Mettez moi au fait, je vous en prie" (Best., XXXIII, 100). As we have seen, d'Alembert's compliance earned him the patriarch's immediate approval (Best., XXXIII, 86). By 1761 d'Alembert feels secure enough in his rôle to upbraid his master for divulging the contents of one of his letters, and to threaten to discontinue sending information if he persists. Noting that he wishes to avoid "des tracasseries," d'Alembert affirms: "C'est pourquoi, si vous voulez savoir les 'nouvelles de l'école,' promettez-moi que vous ne me vendrez plus, et commencez par ne pas parler de ceci" (XLI, 261).

Voltaire's dependence on d'Alembert, however, was not based solely on his value as an informant. Unlike Diderot, who had compromised himself early in his career through his forthright declaration of his views,[1] d'Alembert had been careful to avoid difficulties with the authorities and had thus secured for himself a certain prestige, based first of all on his eminence as a mathematician and augmented by his election to the Académie des Sciences and to the Académie française. His oratorical ability soon made him a favorite speaker at the sessions of the Académie française, which he used as an important sounding board for his views. More than once he had taken the opportunity to praise Voltaire before the Académie as well as in the *Encyclopédie* and in his own *Mélanges*.[2] He had even modified a passage from Voltaire to make it inoffensive to pious ears, and had had it read to the queen herself (XL, 261). When Voltaire was being constantly attacked by his enemies,

1. As early as 1745 Diderot had been denounced to the police by his parish priest. A second denunciation in 1747 placed the author under police surveillance until his arrest in 1749. See Franco Venturi, *Jeunesse de Diderot* (Paris, 1939), p. 170.

2. In 1760, for example, d'Alembert praised Voltaire in both his *Réflexions sur l'histoire* (D'Al., II, 19), and his *Réflexions sur la poésie* (XL, 526). Thereafter he used his position at the Académie more and more to eulogize Voltaire and all "right-minded" authors until, as Pomeau points out: "Si, vers 1770, l'Académie est devenu un bastion du parti, c'est à d'Alembert que Voltaire le doit." *La Religion*, p. 330.

such praise and support, coming from a respectable academician, could mean much in offsetting the adverse effects of these attacks. Voltaire recognized d'Alembert's value as his defender before French public opinion ("Vous me couvrez de votre égide contre les gueules de Cerbères," he told his disciple [XLI, 199]), and, on occasion, called upon his friend to use his influence in his behalf. For example, when in May, 1760, he sought to have his *Eléments de Newton* accepted by the Académie des Sciences, he asked d'Alembert's aid in the project (XL, 397).[3] In 1761 we find him asking for scientific information about the planet Venus, and requesting his friend's support in the Académie française for his forthcoming edition of *Corneille* (XLI, 338, 428). When in 1762 he takes up the defense of the Calas family he asks d'Alembert to echo his cry in the Paris salons and "animate" public opinion (XLII, 168).

Finally, if Voltaire was to be an effective leader of the Philosophe movement he needed a trusted and devoted agent in Paris who not only would keep him informed, but who would himself be a leader. We have seen that Voltaire considered his friend to be the head of the *Encyclopédie*. When d'Alembert resigned his post, Voltaire still considered him the leader and, ironically enough, called Diderot and his aides "cowards" for not following him (Best., XXXIII, 99). Upon discovering in Palissot's preface a quotation from La Mettrie falsely attributed to

3. On 16 June 1760 d'Alembert writes Voltaire: "J'attends votre catéchisme newtonien, et je ne vous ferai pas attendre dès que je l'aurai." In a footnote Moland states: "Nous ne savons quel est l'ouvrage de Voltaire que veut désigner d'Alembert" (XL, 422). The statement may well be in answer to Voltaire's request of 26 May: "Pourriez-vous me rendre un petit service? J'ai fait jadis des *Eléments de Newton* . . . pourrais-je les faire approuver par l'Académie des Sciences?" (XL, 397)

the Encyclopedists, his first thought is of d'Alembert, and he writes Thieriot: "Vous devriez courir chez M. d'Alembert, qui ne sait pas peut-être combien ces passages sont altérés. . . . Je pense qu'il faudrait faire un ouvrage sage, ferme et piquant, où tous les tours de mauvaise foi des ennemis fussent relevés. Qui le peut mieux que M. d'Alembert?" (XL, 413–14). In such a strategic position, d'Alembert had good reason to feel confident of Voltaire's co-operation in his plan, but there was still the task of molding his master to suit his own concepts. As the quotation above indicates, Voltaire conceived his rôle as that of the general deploying his troops from his sheltered headquarters and encouraging them on to battle. This was, however, a rôle which d'Alembert imagined for himself. While he fostered the image of Voltaire as the prophet of the new gospel, with himself as a loyal apostle, in reality he refused to accept the patriarch's plan of campaign and, eventually, won his friend over to his own views.

The policy struggles between Voltaire and d'Alembert, although they are simply facets of the same problem, may be divided into two categories: (1) over-all strategy, and (2) the respective rôles of Voltaire and d'Alembert in this plan. As René Pomeau has pointed out, Voltaire's general plan was to gain the support of "les pouvoirs."[4] If those who controlled the state could be won over to the Philosophe cause, the nation would follow. Thus, he cultivated the friendship, not only of foreign monarchs, but of French nobles such as the minister Choiseul, who might serve to protect the flock by their rank and authority. D'Alembert, and the Philosophes in general, mistrusted the aristocracy and believed that, despite their apparent friendship with

---

4. *La Religion*, p. 315. Naves, p. 164, calls it the "tactique des alliances."

Voltaire, they were basically inimical to the Philosophe cause and could not be relied on for support.[5] The surest means of success, in d'Alembert's opinion, was to gain such a high position of prestige and honor as men of letters that the opposition would no longer dare attack them for fear of appearing unreasonable. Men of letters were the real dispensers of fame, he felt, and could maintain their independence if they had "a noble enough soul" to wish it.[6] The Philosophe party, then, would gain its objectives "sans faire sa cour aux puissances"[7]; however, the help of the ruling aristocracy would not be refused when it was expedient to use it: "Après tout, il est bon que la philosophie fasse flèche de tout bois, et que tout concoure à la

5. D'Alembert sought to remain aloof from and independent of the nobility, whose protection he called "une ressource si triste et si dangereuse." His antipathy toward the great is reflected in his *Essai sur la société des gens de lettres et des grands,* wherein he states: "Le sage, en rendant à la naissance et à la fortune même les devoirs que la société lui prescrit, est en quelque sorte avare de ces devoirs; il les borne à l'extérieur, parce qu'un philosophe sait ménager et non pas encenser les préjugés de sa nation, et qu'il salue les idoles du peuple quand on l'y oblige, mais ne va pas les chercher de lui-même. . . . Le sage n'oublie point surtout que s'il est un respect ex-térieur que les talents doivent aux titres, il en est un autre plus réel que les titres doivent aux talents" (D'Al., IV, 357).

6. *Œuvres et correspondance inédites de d'Alembert,* ed. Charles Henry (Paris, 1887), p. 70.

7. Ibid., p. 73. This attitude had almost prevented d'Alembert's admission into the Académie française. Lucien Brunel describes Mme du Deffand's efforts in his behalf despite his aloofness: ". . . aussi bien d'Alembert se défendait-il fort du rôle de solliciteur: il se complaisait dans celui d'Alceste. Mme de Pompadour, le président Hénault, tous ceux que Mme du Deffand voudrait le voir ménager et séduire, il se les aliène à plaisir. . . . Mme du Deffand fut infatigable: les coups de boutoir de d'Alembert ne l'empêchèrent pas de lui recruter des électeurs." *Les Philosophes et l'Académie française au dix-huitième siècle* (Paris, 1884), pp. 40–41.

servir, même les parlements, qui ne s'en doutent pas, et quelques honnêtes gens, qui la détestent, mais qui, tout en la détestant, lui sont utiles malgré eux" (XLIII, 63).

If the party was to maintain its independence and increase its prestige, it could not openly flaunt the customs and beliefs of the times; rather, it must appear to acquiesce, reserving only the right to plead persuasively for more tolerance toward unbelievers. D'Alembert exposes his plan for a gradual, evolutionary change in the beliefs of his contemporaries in an essay, *Sur la véritable religion*, in which he concludes: "Vouloir trop brusquement éclairer des hommes renfermés dans les ténèbres, c'est non seulement risquer de les aveugler, c'est risquer de leur rendre la lumière odieuse, en leur faisant croire qu'elle est un mal."[8]

The first instance of a divergence in views between Voltaire and d'Alembert regarding "les puissances" was brought out clearly in the controversy resulting from Palissot's play *Les Philosophes*. Raymond Naves has studied in detail the relations between Palissot and Voltaire, underlining the former's attempt to drive a wedge between the patriarch and the Philosophes.[9] We need only touch on the essentials here. When Palissot, a former disciple of Voltaire, sent his master a copy of his new play, Voltaire replied cautiously, knowing that the playwright was protected by influential nobles, particularly Mme de Robecq, an intimate friend of the duc de Choiseul. Inasmuch as abbé Morellet had already been imprisoned for his counterattack against Palissot's satire,[10] Voltaire's re-

8. *Œuvres inéd.*, ed. Henry, p. 8. This approach was to be followed by "des sages qui habiteraient les vastes contrées où l'erreur domine," it should be noted, and not by their defender Voltaire who had "rien à craindre."

9. Naves, pp. 70–86.

10. His *La Vision de Charles Palissot*, by satirizing Mme de Robecq, had angered the duc de Choiseul, who then caused the author to be incarcerated.

luctance to attack Palissot in his usually devastating manner seemed suspect to the Philosophes.[11] He attempted to explain his caution in a letter to d'Alembert dated 10 June 1760, by pointing out the power of Palissot's protectors (XL, 414) and expressing his fear of the consequences for "la bonne cause." The court, he asserts, will say: " 'Palissot est le vengeur des mœurs,' et on coffrera les frères et on aura les philosophes en horreur" (XL, 415).

The Philosophes saw in this affair clear evidence of the weakness in Voltaire's policy of catering to powerful nobles at all costs. Palissot, or any other enemy, might escape his wrath by making sure he had enough protectors at court. In d'Alembert's opinion, any attack, from whatever quarter, must be dealt with by Voltaire without restraint. In a long reply to his friend's letter, d'Alembert calls Mme de Robecq a "méchante femme" who deserved the mention she received in *La Vision* because this "vipère" was instrumental in producing Palissot's *Philosophes*. He then turns to the subject of Voltaire's friends, the duc de Choiseul and Mme du Deffand, and says they are the real cause of Morellet's imprisonment. Finally, he reminds Voltaire that, as their leader, he is responsible for the defense of the Philosophes: "C'est très bien fait au chef de recommander l'union aux frères; mais il faut que le chef reste à leur tête, et il ne faut pas que la crainte d'humilier des polissons protégés l'empêche de parler haut pour la bonne cause, sauf à ménager, s'il le veut, les protecteurs, qui au fond regardent leurs protégés comme des polissons" (XL, 420–21).

Voltaire, in the embarrassing position of seeming to favor his noble friends over his own "troupeau," tried to

11. Voltaire sensed the weakness of his position vis-à-vis the Philosophes and he wrote accordingly to d'Argental: ". . . je dois craindre qu'on ne me reproche d'être complice de la comédie des *Philosophes*" (XL, 406).

repair the damage by writing a more forceful and cate-
gorical letter to Palissot in reply to the latter's "Préface"
attacking the Encyclopedists. He announces this to d'Alembert on 23 June 1760, but it is clear that he has not
abandoned his views concerning the rôle of the nobility
in "the cause." He defends Mme de Robecq and reiterates
that the mention in *La Vision* of this woman, who "never
persecuted any Philosophes," has offended the duc de
Choiseul and was "un coup terrible pour la bonne cause"
(XL, 436).

More than words would now be necessary to convince
the Philosophes that the good will of Choiseul could be
useful to the cause. If Diderot could be accepted in the
Académie française through the good graces of the duke,
there could no longer be any dispute as to the efficacy of
the technique of currying favor with the court. Without
waiting for d'Alembert to reply to his previous letter, Voltaire announces on 9 July his campaign to have Diderot's
candidacy accepted. As if to anticipate his friend's arguments he explains: "Ne croyez point du tout que M. le
duc de Choiseul vous barre; je vous le répète, je ne vous
trompe pas; il se fera un mérite de vous servir, vous et les
penseurs." If Mme de Robecq had not died after the performance of "la Palissoterie," he insists, the author of *La
Vision* would never have gone to the Bastille.[12] And he
concludes: "Il y a très grande apparence qu'il protégera
Diderot" (XL, 452). D'Alembert remained unconvinced.
The Palissot affair had been sufficient proof for him that

12. Morellet, in his *Vision,* had represented Mme de Robecq as
being carried to the first performance of Palissot's *Philosophes* despite
her dying state. She apparently was ignorant of her critical condition,
and the shock of Morellet's revelation was blamed for her death
shortly thereafter. Voltaire is inaccurate, however, when he blames
Morellet's imprisonment on Mme de Robecq's death. According to
the abbé himself, she died "quinze jours après mon emprisonnement."
Abbé Morellet, *Mémoires inédites* (Paris, 1821), I, 93.

the nobles were more likely to be on the side of the enemy, but, rather than pursue the argument further, he simply states that apparently neither of them will change his mind about Palissot's protectors; but he suggests that the observer who is closest to the events is more likely to be correct in his judgment. As to Diderot's entry into the Académie, it is more impossible than Voltaire imagines. His friends might serve him "très mollement," but "les dévots crieraient et l'emporteraient" (XL, 468).

Voltaire refused to have the matter of his aristocratic friend's reliability thus dismissed, however, and dispatched his rebuttal declaring: "Je vous demande pardon, mon très cher philosophe; tout grand homme que vous êtes, c'est vous qui vous trompez, c'est vous qui êtes éloigné, et c'est moi qui suis réellement sur les lieux." And he quotes Choiseul's letter: "On peut donner des coups de bâton à Palissot, je le trouverai fort bon," to show his protector's good will toward the Philosophes (XL, 475–76). Despite his active campaign, Voltaire failed to gain a seat in the Académie for Diderot, who actually resented this unsolicited interference.[13]

A third letter to Palissot in reply to the latter's communication to Voltaire did not help matters. The patriarch had written in a light, bantering tone ending with the suggestion that both sides bury their differences and live amicably together. D'Alembert on 3 August 1760 speaks of the exchange of letters with Palissot and points out: "Vos amis ne sont point contents de votre troisième. Il ne faut pas plaisanter avec de pareilles gens" (XL, 490).[14] The basic problem had obviously not been solved. Voltaire was

13. In a letter to Sophie Volland he states: "A propos de Voltaire, il se plaint à Grimm très amèrement de mon silence: il dit qu'il est au moins de la politesse de remercier son avocat. Et qui diable l'a prié de plaider ma cause?" Roth, III, 247.

14. Diderot refers to "la honte du commerce épistolaire avec Palissot" in a letter to Sophie Volland. Ibid., p. 190.

still intent on remaining in the good graces of "les puissances," and his reply to Thieriot's complaint seemed a
further proof that this preoccupation had inhibited his
loyalty to the cause. On 20 August he writes: "Je pense
que vous êtes trop difficile de blâmer mes réponses à Palissot. Songez qu'il a passé plusieurs jours chez moi, qu'il
m'a été recommandé par ce qu'on appelle les puissances,
et que je lui ai mandé: 'Vous avez tort, et vous devez avoir
des remords'" (XL, 517).

Voltaire's defense of those responsible for Morellet's imprisonment, together with his reluctance to attack Palissot
with the same vigor he was employing against Pompignan *et al.*, left d'Alembert somewhat puzzled at this policy
of appeasement at all costs. He replies to his friend's letter
of 24 July: "Il y a apparence, mon cher et grand philosophe,
que celui de nous deux qui se trompe sur la personne
en question se trompera longtemps: car nous ne paraissons
disposés ni l'un ni l'autre à changer d'avis. Quoi qu'il en
soit, je n'entends rien, je l'avoue, à cette nouvelle juris-
prudence qui permet à une femme de la cour de se mettre
à la tête d'une cabale infâme contre des gens de lettres esti-
mables, et qui ne permet pas aux gens de lettres outragés de
donner un léger ridicule à la protectrice" (XL, 489). This
time Voltaire allowed the matter to drop and gave up
pleading for his friend Choiseul, at least temporarily.

The disapprobation of the Philosophes in Paris, and es-
pecially of d'Alembert, "le plus selon mon cœur" (XL,
532), had left Voltaire on the defensive and, therefore,
more receptive to his friend's suggestions. D'Alembert, for
his part, reinforced his arguments for his method of fighting "the good fight" by giving a forceful eulogy of Voltaire
at the Académie française in his *Réflexions sur la poésie*.
In keeping with his policy of encouraging the friends of
the cause with "le tribut de reconnaissance," he writes the
patriarch suggesting he compose "une statue pour la pos-

térité" in honor of Mlle Clairon because she has done much to further Voltaire's plays, because she has attacked Palissot's *Philosophes,* and because she is, herself, a "philosophe" (XL, 547). In addition, as if to give concrete proof of the success of his method, d'Alembert institutes a ceremony which will become an integral part of the initiation into the "brotherhood" of Philosophes. After the chevalier de Maudave's pilgrimage to Ferney, the geometer sends word that another pilgrim is coming—Turgot, who is a very good "cacouac" but who has good reason to keep it hidden (XLI, 22). Turgot's visit apparently convinced Voltaire of the efficacy of d'Alembert's method. He writes an enthusiastic letter to his disciple praising Turgot and exclaiming: "Travaillez, mon cher Paul, à la vigne du Seigneur. Un homme de votre trempe fait plus de bien que cent sots ne font de mal. C'est un grand plaisir de voir croître son petit troupeau. Vous ne serez point mordu des loups, vous êtes aussi sage qu'intrépide. Vous ne vous commetez point, vous ne jetez la semence que dans le bon terrain. Que Dieu répande ses saintes bénédictions sur vous et les vôtres!" (XLI, 65–66). Three months later Voltaire again writes to his "général" announcing the completion of the requested praise of Mlle Clairon, the *Epître à Daphné,* and thanking him for the renewed praise in his *Réflexions sur l'histoire* given at the Académie on 19 January 1761 (XLI, 199). Interestingly enough, Voltaire returns to the subject of Diderot's candidacy for the Académie, but this time he leaves the decision to d'Alembert: "Nous remettons tout à votre prudence; vous savez agir comme écrire" (XLI, 200).

Having induced Voltaire to accept his approach, d'Alembert now proceeded to implement it more fully. His aim was to identify the Philosophe party with the "hommes de Lettres" so that its enemies would be in the uncomfortable position of attacking the most distinguished literary figures of the age. Thus, Voltaire was constantly praised by d'Alembert not for his works attacking the abuses of the old régime but for his purely literary works. Voltaire was the great poet, the great dramatist, the great defender of French good taste, etc. Conversely, Voltaire was called upon to add his already famous name to that of d'Alembert to reward their younger disciples for good work in the cause or to encourage those who had shown good will toward the Philosophes to continue to do so. An example of this "commerce d'encens," as Fréron called it,[15] is d'Alembert's request to Voltaire upon the publication of Morellet's *Manuel des Inquisiteurs*. He writes the patriarch on 27 January 1762: "Comme il faut encourager les gens de bien, écrivez-moi, je vous prie, un mot d'honnêteté pour cet honnête ecclésiastique: il le mérite par son zèle pour la bonne cause, et par son respect pour vous" (XLII, 23). Similarly, he asks Voltaire to write to M. le prince Louis de Rohan to thank him for his good will toward "les gens de lettres," and suggests he do so in verse for a better effect (XLIII, 88). The effectiveness of this technique is illustrated by Rohan's reaction to Voltaire's letter of praise. D'Alembert tells the patriarch that "prince Louis" is delighted with it and is showing it to everybody (XLIII, 137).[16] Another means of strengthening the party's position was afforded d'Alembert through his influence in the Académie française. By backing "right-minded" candidates against the "cabale des dévots" he succeeded gradually in making the respected Académie a bastion of Philosophe thought, so that Voltaire could rightly say: "On ambitionne votre suffrage, et il me semble que vous jouez un

15. *L'Année littéraire,* I, 14.
16. Recipients of Voltaire's letters were proud of this honor and shared them with friends. Mlle de Lespinasse, for example, tells of going to the home of Duplessis, the painter, where d'Argental read them a letter just received from the patriarch, and, she continues:

assez beau rôle. Vous êtes comme les anciens enchanteurs, qui faisaient la destinée des hommes avec des paroles" (XLIII, 49).[17]

".. . je l'ai trouvée si bonne, le ton en est si doux, si naturel, on est si près de lui en le lisant, que . . . j'ai demandé cette lettre. J'ai demandé d'en prendre une copie, dans ce moment on l'a fait, et mon ami la lira." *Lettres de Mlle de Lespinasse,* ed. G. Isambert (Paris, 1876), I, 161.

17. The statement of d'Alembert's method and evaluation of its success is necessarily sketchy here, since only those details are given which are pertinent to this subject. A more thorough exposition and documentation will be made in my forthcoming study on d'Alembert.

Policy Clashes

THREE

W HILE VOLTAIRE at times appeared to concur whole-
heartedly in d'Alembert's views, he was still not convinced of the desirability of compromise with the enemy.
He had hoped, by his own example, to inspire his followers
to an active campaign of bold, devastating attacks published anonymously so as to "écraser l'Infâme" without
exposing themselves to prosecution. When he was actively
engaged in the encyclopedic venture, Voltaire, although
he furnished the articles requested of him, had frequently
expressed his dissatisfaction with the *Encyclopédie* precisely because its authors could not express their views
openly and forcefully. In 1756, for example, he had
written d'Alembert: "Ce qu'on m'a dit des articles de
la théologie et de la métaphysique me serre le cœur. Il
est bien cruel d'imprimer le contraire de ce qu'on
pense" (Best., XXX, 160–61).[1] The difficulties experi-

1. Pierre-Georges Castex and Paul Surer, in their *Manuel des
études littéraires françaises* (Paris, 1949), IV, 104, assert that Voltaire
lost his enthusiasm for the *Encyclopédie* "quand il se vit confondre
dans la foule des collaborateurs"; but I find no evidence to justify
this view.

enced by the editors of the publication after the appearance of the article "Genève," and the imprisonment in 1760 of Morellet for writing *La Vision,* underlined the truth of d'Alembert's reply that with censorship and a "privilège" to consider, it was the best they could do (Best., XXXI, 237). Voltaire's solution would have been to publish clandestinely and anonymously, but, because of the unfavorable reaction of the Philosophes to his rôle in the Palissot affair, there seemed little choice but to follow d'Alembert's lead. Had the latter not made this clear when he indignantly retorted to Voltaire's complaint about the inaction of the Philosophes? It was up to him to defend the Philosophes since he was out of reach of the authorities (XL, 380).

Voltaire needed no encouragement, as the flood of brochures he produced at this time attests, but he would have liked his disciple to share his zeal. After a year of silence on the matter, he returns to the subject with a new approach. Instead of a stinging reprimand, he now tries coaxing his friend: "Allons donc, rendez quelque service au genre humain; écrasez le fanatisme, sans pourtant risquer de tomber, comme Samson, sous les ruines du temple qu'il démolit. . . . Je ne connais que vous qui puissiez venger la raison. . . . Faites-moi ce plaisir avant que je meure" (XLI, 293–94). This time d'Alembert ignored the plea completely, and Voltaire once again resigned himself to the rôle of defender of the flock, asking for the names of those to be attacked (XLII, 79). D'Alembert gladly obliged. Almost every letter to Voltaire thereafter mentions some enemy against whom he urges the master to write a pamphlet. In March, 1762, he notes a parish priest named Le Roy who is to be remembered "à la première bonne digestion que vous aurez" (XLII, 82). His next letter mentions Vernet's *Lettres critiques d'un voyageur anglais* as deserving some recognition (XLII, 99), but, for the moment, he seems less eager for Voltaire's brochures: the Jesuits are being suppressed by the Parlement and he is overjoyed that "tous ces imbéciles, qui croient servir la religion, servent la raison sans s'en douter." Recalling Voltaire's repeated requests for active participation in the struggle, d'Alembert declares that "l'Infâme" is now crushing itself and they need only let it rush to its own destruction. Everything looks rosy, he admits, and he can already foresee "les jansénistes mourant l'année prochaine de leur belle mort, après avoir fait périr cette année-ci les jésuites de mort violente, la tolérance s'établit, les protestants rappelés, les prêtres mariés, la confession abolie, et l'infâme écrasée sans qu'on s'en aperçoive" (XL, 101).[2]

Voltaire was less optimistic and preferred to help the process along by publishing an expurgated version of Meslier's *Testament*. The Calas affair, occurring as it did during this same period, no doubt reinforced his conviction that action was necessary and gave added impetus to his call to arms. He asks d'Alembert to "crier et faire crier" about the "horrible" Calas adventure, and returns more forcefully to his recurrent grievance by chiding his disciple for not echoing his own *Extrait des Sentiments de J. Meslier:* "Jean Meslier doit convertir la terre. Pourquoi son évangile est-il en si peu de mains? Que vous êtes tièdes à Paris! vous laissez la lumiere sous le boisseau"

2. This optimistic mood was to be short lived. Two months later (31 July 1762) d'Alembert is less sure of his prediction: "Enfin le 6 du moi prochain la canaille parlementaire nous délivrera de la canaille jésuitique; mais la raison en sera-t-elle mieux, et l'"inf . . .' plus mal?" (XLII, 191). Voltaire did not share d'Alembert's joy in seeing the Jesuits suppressed. Fearing the Jansenists even more he writes: "Les jésuites étaient nécessaires, ils faisaient diversion; on se moquait d'eux, et on va être écrasé par des pédants qui n'inspireront que l'indignation" (XLIII, 185).

(XLII, 168). The perennial debate was on again, and d'Alembert's rebuttal begins to sound familiar: "Vous nous reprochez de la tiédeur; mais, je crois vous l'avoir déjà dit, la crainte des fagots est très rafraîchissante." The printing and circulation in Paris of the *Testament de Jean Meslier* would do little good, he insists, and even those who agreed with it would consider the Philosophes fools for releasing it (XLII,191). True to his theory that prejudices cannot be destroyed by attacking them openly (D'Al., IV, 304), d'Alembert again spells out his views to the patriarch: "Le genre humain n'est aujourd'hui plus éclairé que parce qu'on a eu la précaution ou le bonheur de ne l'éclairer que peu à peu. Si le soleil se montrait tout à coup dans une cave, les habitants ne s'apercevraient que du mal qu'il leur ferait aux yeux; l'excès de lumière ne serait bon qu'à les aveugler sans ressources. J.-C. doit être attaqué, comme Pierre Corneille, avec ménagement" (XLII, 191).

Voltaire could be as intransigent as d'Alembert. He was still not convinced. It seemed obvious, further, that there was no hope of inspiring his lieutenant to a more active part in the struggle against "l'Infâme." Perhaps a new and more zealous agent to replace this intractable disciple might be the answer. The moment was propitious: d'Alembert was even now in Prussia and there was talk of his remaining at Frederick's court to head his academy. A letter from Helvétius announcing an English translation of his *De l'esprit* must have seemed a providential coincidence to Voltaire. Helvétius had been an early disciple of Voltaire.[3] What was more, he had demonstrated

3. Albert Keim, *Helvétius: sa vie et son œuvre* (Paris, 1907), p. 432, states that "les rapports de Voltaire avec Helvétius avaient été fort étroits. L'illustre écrivain avait patronné les essais poétiques et philosophiques du brillant fermier-général. . . . Mais ces rapports avaient dû être ensuite moins suivis." There are at least twenty-four letters

his courage and zeal by boldly, if imprudently, signing his name to his work. Perhaps with a little guidance he might be groomed as d'Alembert's replacement. Two weeks after receiving the latter's restatement of policy, Voltaire writes to Helvétius to suggest he continue the good work he began with *De l'esprit,* but expresses regret that the book appeared in his own name, because it made him some enemies at the court. Outlining his view as to how the Philosophes should fight their enemies, he stipulates that the king must be convinced that the brothers love his "person" and his "crown" and that they would be incapable of fomenting dissension against him; and, as if in answer to d'Alembert's admonitions that the enemy must be attacked "avec ménagement," the patriarch urges Helvétius to think and write freely because "liberty is a gift of God." But, of course, "il ne faut jamais rien donner sous son nom" (XLII, 207).

Without waiting for a reply, Voltaire repeats his call to action on 25 August (XLII, 557), and, his enthusiasm having reached its peak, he reveals on 15 September his plan to make Helvétius the focal point for uniting the brothers. Reiterating the need for forceful, unrestrained attacks on their enemies, he cites the example of the effect of his own brochures against Lefranc de Pompignan when the latter had insulted the Philosophes in his initial *Discours* at the Académie française. If he had not been confounded, the patriarch asserts, it would have become the fashion at the Académie to vilify the Philosophes. As long as the "gens de bien" are united, no one will dare attack them. It will be up to Helvétius to effect this unity.

---

from Voltaire to Helvétius between 1738 and 1749. For the next ten years the correspondence ceases. With the publication of *De l'esprit* in 1758 the exchanges are renewed. See Chapter V in the present study for Voltaire's reaction to *De l'esprit.*

There follow admonitions as to the plan to follow in fighting for the cause: the brothers must convince the monarch that their "morale" is superior to that of their enemies and is the best guide for the state. Therefore, attacks must always be made anonymously so as not to compromise the party. Then Voltaire explains how he conceives the rôle of Helvétius in his plan: he will organize a salon in his home which is to be the meeting place of the faithful and from which will emanate unsigned publications against "l'Infâme." And he concludes: "Personne n'est plus fait que vous pour réunir les gens de lettres; vous pouvez élever chez vous un tribunal qui sera fort supérieur, chez les honnêtes gens, à celui d'Omer Joly. Vivez gaiement, travaillez utilement, soyez l'honneur de notre patrie. Le temps est venu où les hommes comme vous doivent triompher" (XLII, 571).

It is quite probable that the choice of Helvétius as d'Alembert's successor was an attempt to draw the Diderot circle into closer co-operation with the Voltairian faction. The year before, the preface of Boulanger's *Recherches sur l'origine du despotisme oriental* had been dedicated to Helvétius. This may have suggested to the patriarch that Helvétius already had a respected position within his coterie and might easily be made a focal point for the group. Boulanger's work represented for Voltaire a dangerous trend (see Chapter V). Such an antimonarchical trend might be curbed if Helvétius were won over to the Ferney gospel. Having made up his mind to effect the reconciliation between the two groups in this manner, Voltaire, in his characteristic fashion, spared no effort in the attempt. Despite Helvétius' silence, he reiterates his appeal a few weeks later (XLIII, 4–5), and on the same day he writes to Damilaville asking him to enlist Diderot's aid in convincing his friend Helvétius of the importance and necessity of his writing to avenge "outraged virtue."

He is learned, and has time and money: "Voilà ce que votre ami devrait lui représenter" (XLIII, 3).

Neither Helvétius nor Diderot nor Damilaville responded to these appeals. It was apparent that the group would not be so easily won over. Meanwhile d'Alembert had returned to Paris and there seemed little choice but to continue to rely on this overly cautious lieutenant. Perhaps with enough coaxing he would become more active. On 28 September 1763 Voltaire makes a further attempt to elicit a brochure from his disciple: "Vous enfouissez vos talents; vous vous contentez de mépriser un monstre qu'il faut abhorrer et détruire. Que vous coûterait-il de l'écraser en quatre pages, en ayant la modestie de lui laisser ignorer qu'il meurt de votre main?" (XLII, 583). D'Alembert's reply was brief and familiar: "Vous avez raison; je suis bien peu zélé, et je me le reproche, mais songez donc que le bon sens est emprisonné dans le pays que j'habite" (XLIII, 8). Voltaire complains to Damilaville about it: "Frère Protagoras se contente de rire de l''infâme,' il ne l'écrase pas, et il faut l'écraser" (XLIII, 21).[4]

The successful entry of Marmontel into the Académie française gave d'Alembert an opportunity once more to assume the offensive. Accordingly, he informed Voltaire that although an attempt had been made to keep Marmontel out because he was a Philosophe, the patriarch now had an added partisan within the Académie. Here was visible proof of the effectiveness of his method. D'Alembert presses his advantage by reiterating his concept of their respective rôles in the struggle against the enemy: "Il faut, mon cher maître, que chacun de nous serve la bonne cause suivant ses petits moyens. Vous la servez de votre plume,

4. Voltaire tries from time to time to influence d'Alembert through Damilaville. On 13 December 1763, for example, he writes: "Excitez bien vivement le zèle de Protagoras" (XLIII, 48). See also XLIII, 183, 349.

et moi, à qui on n'en laisserait pas une sur le dos si j'en faisais autant, je tâche de lui gagner des partisans dans le pays ennemi; et ces partisans ne seront point compromis, parce qu'ils ne doivent jamais l'être; mais ils recevront de moi, de tous mes amis, et ils devraient recevoir de vous, le tribut de reconnaissance que tous les êtres pensants leur doivent" (XLIII, 45).

Undoubtedly, Voltaire's ideal would have been to sow dragon's teeth and reap a harvest of lesser Voltaires. He seemed incapable of conceiving any other method but his own in dealing with his adversaries; yet the basic weakness in his approach was that there was only one Voltaire, and, his detailed instructions to Helvétius notwithstanding, his satirical talent could not readily be farmed out to his disciples. D'Alembert himself points this out to the master when the latter urges him to counterattack Jean-Georges Lefranc, the bishop of Puy, for his insults against the Philosophes in his "Instruction pastorale." His method would have to be a serious rebuttal, he explains, which would serve only to give his adversary an existence, and he adds: ". . . des plaisanteries auraient mal réussi, surtout après les vôtres" (XLIII, 63). As if to point out that Voltaire's is not the only solution, d'Alembert asks that he be spared the accusation of having failed the party and insists: ". . . personne peut-être ne lui rend de plus grands services que moi."[5] Then, by way of proof, he reports Marmontel's recent speech before the Académie in

---

5. D'Alembert's words are no empty boast. Frédéric Masson notes that through "l'espèce de dictature qu'il affecta et qui fit du salon de Mlle de Lespinasse l'obligatoire antichambre de l'Académie," d'Alembert "eut peut-on dire une influence singulièrement grave sur la France entière." *L'Académie française, 1629–1793* (Paris, 1912), pp. 44–45. Similarly, Brunel attests to d'Alembert's important rôle in the Académie, saying: "Avec d'Alembert elle devint pour les philosophes, non plus seulement une place de sûreté, mais une citadelle avancée." *Les Philosophes et l'Académie*, p. 29.

praise of Voltaire and concludes: "Je me flatte, comme vous que c'est une acquisition pour la bonne cause. Petit à petit l'Eglise de Dieu se fortifie" (XLIII, 63).

Whether Voltaire liked it or not, d'Alembert had firmly delineated their respective rôles: the master was to defend the party with his pen, while his disciple recruited new members and increased their prestige. His reply to d'Alembert's latest epistle indicated that he knew full well his disciple would not change his stand, "parce que je sais que les philosophes sont têtus" (XLIII, 126).[6] The question still remained as to how d'Alembert should accomplish his self-chosen rôle of acquiring prominence for the Philosophes. The debate on this problem had conveniently been shelved after the Palissot affair but, having been forced to concede one point, Voltaire now turned to the original argument. The alternatives in question had been succinctly stated by d'Alembert in his acceptance speech before the Académie française: "Les lettres ne peuvent être dignement protégées que par les rois, ou par elles-mêmes" (D'Al., IV, 309). There was no doubt as to his own choice. One was either a "courtisan" or a "philosophe"—the two were incompatible.[7] Voltaire, despite the

6. Although these words actually refer to d'Alembert's opinion that Voltaire's reference to Jews as tolerant in his *Traité de la tolérance* was inaccurate, they indicate that the patriarch knew his disciple's character and had no illusions about changing him. They could apply equally to Voltaire himself. In the face of this admission of impotence to sway d'Alembert, he is still trying five days later to force a brochure from him against Crevier: "C'est à vous de venger la raison outragée" (XLIII, 132–33). D'Alembert replied: "Que je confonde, dites-vous, ce maraud de Crevier? Je m'en garderai bien; je n'ai pas d'envie d'être au pilori ou exilé" (XLIII, 180).

7. In 1752 d'Alembert showed his disapproval of Duclos's attempts to be accepted by the "grand monde" by writing to Mme du Deffand: "Mais de quoi s'avise-t-il aussi de vouloir être à la fois courtisan et philosophe? Cela ne saurait aller ensemble." *Correspondance complète de la Marquise du Deffand,* ed. Lescure (Paris, 1865), I, 156.

Palissot experience, persisted in his view that the king and his ministers must be won over. Conceding that d'Alembert's activity in Paris is doing more good than Jansenism and Molinism have done evil, he tells his disciple that the king must be convinced that the Philosophes are his best defenders and urges him to train his sights on young men destined to fill high positions. He then concludes: "Enfin, telle est notre situation, que nous sommes l'exécration du genre humain si nous n'avons pas pour nous les honnêtes gens; il faut donc les avoir, à quelque prix que ce soit; travaillez donc à la vigne, 'écrasez l'inf———.' Que ne pouvez vous faire sans vous compromettre? ne laissez pas une si belle chandelle sous le boisseau" (XLIII, 127).

Other than the suggestion that Mme du Deffand is in reality more favorable to Fréron than to Voltaire, d'Alembert does not pursue the debate further but, rather, expounds his own views on spreading tolerance. Reiterating his contention that it is useless to tell a fanatic he is absurd or atrocious, he pleads for a more subtle method:

Mon avis serait donc de faire à ces pauvres chrétiens beaucoup de politesses, de leur dire qu'ils ont raison, que ce qu'ils croient et ce qu'ils prêchent est clair comme le jour, qu'il est impossible que tout le monde ne finisse par penser comme eux; mais qu'attendu la vanité et l'opiniâtreté humaine, il est bon de permettre à chacun de penser ce qu'il voudra, et qu'ils auront bientôt le plaisir de voir tout le monde de leur avis; qu'à la vérité il s'en damnera bien quelques-uns en chemin jusqu'au moment marqué par Dieu le père pour cette conviction et réunion universelle, mais qu'il faut sacrifier quelques passagers pour mener tout le reste à bon port. Voilà, mon cher et grand philosophe, sauf votre meilleur avis, comme je voudrais plaider notre cause commune.

D'Alembert then reminds the master that he is working

very hard in the meantime to increase the prestige of "le troupeau" and has, in fact, just had Helvétius and the chevalier de Jaucourt elected to the Berlin Academy (XLIII, 136).

Voltaire refused to be sidetracked into a discussion of whether his *Traité de tolérance* was too blunt in tone. There are other ways to preach tolerance, he concedes, "Mais venons au fait." Tolerance is a state matter, and those at the head of the realm are more tolerant than ever. A new generation is rising which detests fanaticism, he continues, and the top places will one day be occupied by Philosophes: the "reign of reason" is imminent. He then defends his friendship with Mme du Deffand by declaring: "Pourvu que la vigne du Seigneur aille bien, je suis indulgent pour les pécheurs et les pécheresses. Je ne connais rien de sérieux que la culture de la vigne; je vous la recommande; provignez, mon cher philosophe, provignez" (XLIII, 145).

Voltaire chose poorly the moment to reopen the discussion on the value of courting "les puissances." He had just vaunted to d'Alembert the tolerance of those at the head of the realm when, as luck would have it, Palissot chose that same time to publish a poem, *La Dunciade*, in which Diderot was severely attacked. Once again the patriarch was in the awkward position of trying to explain away Choiseul's protection of this enemy of the Philosophes. When first informed of the poem by Damilaville, Voltaire tries to belittle it saying that it is too insipid to be influential. The author's protectors wish to be amused, he adds, but they will be disappointed. Then, as he did in his predicament over *Les Philosophes* four years earlier, he tries to show his zeal for Diderot by exclaiming: "Mon ambition est qu'il soit de l'Académie; il faut absolument qu'on le propose pour la première place vacante. Tous les gens de lettres seront pour lui, et il sera très aisé de lui concilier

les personnes de la cour, qui obtiendront pour lui l'approbation du roi" (XLIII, 161–62). Without waiting for an
answer he writes again to Damilaville two days later
(XLIII, 165), and finally, a week later, with still no reply,
he continues to press his defense of Choiseul for protecting
Palissot: the minister is intelligent and loves "philosophy."
We must pardon him for his severity toward Morellet a
few years ago, he suggests, and he concludes with a reaffirmation of his basic position: "Je suis persuadé que tous
nos chers philosophes, en se conduisant bien, en n'affectant
point de braver les puissances de ce monde, trouveront
toujours beaucoup de protection" (XLIII, 170).[8]

It is interesting to note that Voltaire refrained from making the same declarations to d'Alembert. If Damilaville
would accept them in respectful silence, the patriarch already knew d'Alembert's position too well to think he
would let them go unchallenged. Perhaps too, he knew that
Damilaville would show his pronouncements to "Protagoras." In any event, d'Alembert was not long in mentioning *La Dunciade*, whose author had been praised at the
court and protected and rewarded for having represented
respectable persons as "cartouchiens." He shows his disdain

8. Brunel upholds Voltaire's position as basically sound: "Plutôt
favorables à leur parti qu'au parti contraire, Mme de Pompadour et
M. de Choiseul ne demandaient qu'à les laisser faire, pourvu qu'ils ne
se compromissent pas. C'est ce que Voltaire répétait sans cesse à ses
amis parfois un peu défiants." *Les Philosophes et l'Académie*, pp.
177–78. Pomeau, on the other hand, when discussing Voltaire's attempt
to reconcile the Philosophes with "le cercle des Choiseul" comments:
"Peine perdue; Choiseul et son entourage, particulièrement Mme du
Deffand gardent rancune aux encyclopédistes." *La Religion*, p. 316.
Both views contain an element of truth. Choiseul might have been
willing to look more favorably on the Philosophes if d'Alembert had
abandoned his proud posture of defying "les puissances" and had been
more conciliatory, but, as Voltaire wrote him: ". . . vous n'êtes pas
homme à faire les avances" (XLIV, 242).

for the protection of those "personnes illustres" by pointing out its ineffectiveness. Palissot, he notes, had also insulted Crevier in his *Dunciade*. The "old Jansenist" complained to the Parlement, and Palissot's protectors had their protégé exiled to avoid difficulties with the Parlement. "Dites après cela que les lettres ne sont pas favorisées," he adds sarcastically (XLIII, 179). The event served to prove once more to d'Alembert what he had once told his master in referring to Diderot's entry into the Académie: even if Voltaire's friends were willing to help, it would be "très mollement," and the "dévots" would have their way (XL, 468). It was evident to d'Alembert that the party must rely on its own merits rather than lose its freedom through a debasing dependence on questionable protectors.[9] Finally, as if to underscore his contempt for Voltaire's noble friends, he concludes that if he were writing a *Dunciade* he would not choose Palissot's targets but more illustrious names (XLIII, 179). Voltaire, no less intransigent, retorted: "A l'égard des hauts lieux dont vous me parlez, sachez que ceux qui habitent ces hauts lieux sont philosophes, sont tolérants, et dé-

9. The fear of losing his freedom of action had been one reason for d'Alembert's refusal to go to Frederick's court. In discussing his refusal with Mme du Deffand he states: "Je resterai à Paris, j'y mangerai du pain et des noix, j'y mourrai pauvre, mais aussi j'y vivrai libre." Du Deffand, *Corres. complète,* ed. Lescure, I, 155. Cousin d'Avalon, p. 129, states of this trait: "L'amour de d'Alembert pour l'indépendance allait jusqu'au fanatisme, au point qu'il se refusait souvent à des choses qui lui auraient été agréables, lorsqu'il prévoyait qu'elles pourraient être pour lui l'origine de quelque contrainte; ce qui fit dire avec raison à un de ses amis, qu'il était 'esclave de sa liberté.' " According to Desnoiresterres, this tendency might be attributed to d'Alembert's humble beginnings and difficult childhood, which taught him "qu'il ne fallait attendre des autres que le moins possible, que tout dépendait de la patience, d'une volonté énergique sans emportement et sans colère, et d'un travail opiniâtre." *Voltaire et la société*, V, 159.

testent les intolérants, avec lesquels ils sont obligés de vivre" (XLIII, 185). The very next day (15 April 1763), one of those living in "ces hauts lieux," Mme de Pompadour, passed away. The loss of this "protectrice assurée" (XLIII, 203) was a blow to Voltaire's plans, and seemed to close the discussion for the time being. By way of epitaph, he writes of her to d'Alembert: "Dans le fond de son cœur elle était des nôtres; elle protégeait les lettres autant qu'elle le pouvait: voilà un beau rêve de fini" (XLIII, 205).

* * * * *

D'Alembert was not one to forget an injury. He might seem to overlook it when convenient, but it was only to await a more favorable occasion to repay it. Thus, when Vernet attacked him in his *Lettres critiques d'un voyageur anglais,* the Philosophe wrote to Voltaire: "Il me serait bien aise de le couvrir de ridicules, mais c'est un honneur que je ne juge pas à propos de lui faire. Peut-être cependant trouverai-je occasion de lui donner quelque jour une légère marque de reconnaissance" (XLII, 99). It may well be that such an insult was at the base of his almost obsessive desire to make his way independently of aristocratic protectors, and particularly of the duc de Choiseul.[10] His frequent

10. When he tells Mme du Deffand on 4 December 1752 that he has decided to stay in France he adds: "Ce n'est pas que je sois fort content du ministère, et surtout de l'ami [Choiseul?], ou soi-disant tel, de votre président [Hénault]: il s'en faut beaucoup. Je sais, à n'en pouvoir douter, qu'il est très mal disposé pour moi, et j'ignore absolument pour quelle raison: mais que m'importe?" Du Deffand, *Corres. complète,* ed. Lescure, I, 155. It may be that at some time d'Alembert had been assured of financial success if he would praise the minister. In a letter to the Marquis d'Argens dated 16 September 1752 he says he is "oublié du gouvernement," and "persécuté même autant qu'on peut l'être quand on évite de donner trop d'avantage sur soi à la

harassment of Voltaire for maintaining a correspondence with Mme du Deffand (XLIII, 137, 179, 336; XLIV, 41, 237; XLVII, 130), doubtlessly motivated by his rift with her over Mlle de Lespinasse and aggravated by her leanings toward Fréron, is a further illustration of this tendency to harbor a grudge indefinitely.[11]

The suppression of the Jesuits in 1762 and the more severe measures enacted against them in 1764 were to bring to the fore one of d'Alembert's strongest resentments. As we have seen, Jesuit opposition had been an important factor in the suppression of the *Encyclopédie*. D'Alembert had already shown his contempt for the Society and for its organ, the *Journal de Trévoux*, in the "Avertissement" of Volume III of the *Encyclopédie*,[12] and, even after their expulsion from France, he sought unsuccessfully to have them

---

méchanceté des hommes," and he adds: "Je n'ai aucune part aux récompenses qui pleuvent ici sur les gens de lettres avec plus de profusion que de lumières" (D'Al., V, 17). In 1765 d'Alembert suggests Choiseul's protection of Palissot's *Les Philosophes* as one reason for not wishing to owe anything to the minister (XLIV, 40). The investigation of d'Alembert's deep resentment toward the "grand seigneur" will be pursued more thoroughly in my forthcoming study.

11. In 1766 when David Hume had given d'Alembert the liberty to edit the *Exposé succinct* of his quarrel with J.-J. Rousseau, d'Alembert had censured Horace Walpole's satirical letter against Rousseau as "cruelle." Hume later wrote to Walpole: "What could engage d'Alembert to use this freedom I cannot imagine. Is it possible that a man of his superior parts can bear you ill will because you are the friend of his enemy, Madame du Deffand? What makes me suspect that there may be something true of this suspicion, is, that several passages in my narrative, in which I mention you and that letter, are all altered in the translation, and rendered much less obliging than I wrote them." *The Letters of David Hume*, ed. Greig (Oxford, 1932), II, 101. For Walpole's reply see *The Letters of Horace Walpole*, ed. Toynbee (Oxford, 1904), VII, 69–71.

12. See my *Berthier's Journal de Trévoux*, pp. 134–36, 189–90, for details of d'Alembert's attitude toward the Jesuits.

driven from Silesia through his influence with Frederick II of Prussia (XLIII, 63, 180). Despite his policy of refraining from writing on controversial matters, d'Alembert began "quelques réflexions fort simples sur l'embarras où les jésuites se trouvent entre leur souverain et leur général," but, he added prudently in a letter to Voltaire, he would wait until they had gone, "pour me moquer d'eux" (XLIII, 146). Voltaire showed enough interest in the project to offer the suggestion that it be published anonymously (XLIII, 206), but surprisingly enough, he did not pursue the matter any further. Perhaps it was because he was not so anxious as d'Alembert to see the Jesuits expelled from France. As he pointed out to his friend two months later: "Je souhaite de tout mon cœur qu'il reste des jésuites en France; tant qu'il y en aura, les jansénistes et eux s'égorgeront: les moutons, comme vous savez, respirent un peu quand les loups et les renards se déchirent" (XLIII, 276).

A further reason for Voltaire's apparent neglect of d'Alembert's plan for an anti-Jesuit work may have been due to his distraction at this time by two pressing preoccupations. On 28 May, in his *Lettres de la Montagne*, Rousseau had attacked the patriarch as his most violent persecutor; Voltaire, in turn, instituted an intensive campaign of denials.[13] Further, the repercussions from his own *Dictionnaire philosophique* had alarmed Voltaire and had caused him to write persistently to his friends begging them to second his denials of authorship (XLIII, 273, 276, 289, 307, 314, 317, 318–20, 322, 323, 326, 329, 331, 332, 333, 337, 338, 344, 345).

It may also be that he was less interested in pursuing a group already eliminated from the battle and would have

13. See my "Rousseau and d'Alembert," *PMLA*, LXXV (March, 1960), 46–60, for details on Voltaire's attacks against Rousseau and d'Alembert's attempts to attenuate them.

been more enthusiastic if d'Alembert had proposed to use his pen to attack the enemies who remained. This is borne out by Voltaire's reopening of the question of his friend's rôle in the struggle against their common enemy. When abbé Saas attacks the editors of the *Encyclopédie* in his *Lettres sur l'"Encyclopédie,"* reprinting at the same time the official condemnation made at the time of its suppression, Voltaire asks Damilaville for the names of "les gadouards" who wrote this attack. He then reveals his exasperation with d'Alembert for refusing to participate more actively in the struggle. He should stop whatever he is doing and write something useful for the cause: "Il est comme Achille qui a quitté le camp des Grecs; mais il est temps qu'il s'arme et qu'il reprenne sa lance. Je l'en prie comme le bon homme Phœnix, et je vous prie de vous joindre à moi" (XLIII, 349). Four days later he writes d'Alembert and tells him that the *Lettres sur l'"Encyclopédie"* have attacked him, begging him to write a rebuttal but without revealing his identity (XLIII, 351).

By 9 November 1764 d'Alembert had still not replied to his friend's appeal, but Voltaire had not yet given up hope. He writes to Damilaville: "Je ne sais pourquoi frère Protagoras ne m'écrit point; je n'en compte pas moins sur son zèle fraternel" (XLIII, 370), and on the same day he repeats his plea to d'Alembert to write something for the cause (XLIII, 371). D'Alembert's reply has not been preserved, but Voltaire's letter of 19 December referring to the receipt of his note (XLIII, 404) leads one to believe that the geometer must have pointed to the completed manuscript of his *Sur la destruction des jésuites* as proof of his literary activity against "l'Infâme." Apparently d'Alembert had asked Voltaire to arrange for the printing of the manuscript in Geneva through the latter's own publisher, Cramer, because a week later Voltaire announces receipt of the manuscript and tells his disciple that Cramer will send him the money for it (XLIII, 413).[14]

The *Destruction* must have been a pleasant surprise for Voltaire. What his constant pleading had failed to do, d'Alembert's lingering resentment of the Jesuits had accomplished.[15] For the first time, he had dared to be bold. Voltaire expresses his joy to Damilaville, exclaiming: "Que j'aime sa précision, sa force, et sa plaisanterie! qu'il est sage et hardi!" (XLIII, 410). And in a note included in Damilaville's letter for his "Archimède-Protagoras," he tells d'Alembert: "Je ne connais rien de plus sage et de plus fort; vous êtes le prêtre de la raison, qui enterrez le fanatisme. . . . Dieu vous bénisse! Dieu vous le rende! Vous écrasez, en vous jouant, les molinistes, les jansénistes; vous faites le bien de l'Etat en rendant méprisables les deux partis qui l'ont troublé. . . . On a lapidé les jésuites avec les pierres des décombres de Port-Royal; vous lapidez les convulsionnaires avec les ruines du tombeau du diacre Pâris, et la fronde dont vous lancez vos cailloux va jusqu'à Rome frapper le nez du pape" (XLIII, 413).

It is evident here that Voltaire is overjoyed not so much because d'Alembert has attacked the Jesuits, but because he has dared attack with equal vigor those still to be dealt with. It is equally clear from d'Alembert's reply that if he has not struck out heretofore it was not because of indiffer-

14. Voltaire's *Lettres inédites à son imprimeur Gabriel Cramer*, ed. Gagnebin (Genève, 1952), reveal the effort and time expended by Voltaire in acting as d'Alembert's agent in the publication of *Sur la destruction des jésuites*. The solicitude he showed for the satisfaction of his friend's request is a good indication of the extent of his regard for d'Alembert.

15. In describing d'Alembert's reluctance to compromise himself for the cause, Pomeau adds: "Mais la haine de l'Eglise, qui dévore ce fils d'une religieuse, l'emporte habituellement sur sa prudence." *La Religion*, p. 330. While I would question the term "habituellement," this statement is certainly applicable in the case of the *Destruction*.

ence to the cause. With an intensity that is rare for the geometer, he shows, in answer to Voltaire's enthusiastic praise, his burning hatred for "l'Infâme," and his satisfaction at having finally given it expression:

Je ne vous le dissimule point, mon cher maître; vous me comblez de satisfaction par tout ce que vous me dites de mon ouvrage. Je le recommande à votre protection, et je crois qu'en effet il pourra être utile à la cause commune, et que "l'infâme," avec toutes les révérences que je fais semblant de lui faire, ne s'en trouvera pas mieux. Si j'étais comme vous, assez loin de Paris pour lui donner des coups de bâton, assurément ce serait de tout mon cœur, de tout mon esprit, et de toutes mes forces, comme on prétend qu'il faut aimer Dieu; mais je ne suis posté que pour lui donner des croquignoles, en lui demandant pardon de la liberté grande, et il me semble que je ne m'en suis pas mal acquitté. [XLIII, 422]

The success of his *Destruction,* untarnished by the "tracasseries" he had feared would result, along with its enthusiastic reception by the Philosophes and particularly by Voltaire, seems to have encouraged d'Alembert to abandon his former policy and to try his hand again in the same genre. He announces to Voltaire that he is tired of submitting his works to the censors and he hopes that Cramer handles his *Destruction* satisfactorily because he plans to send more brochures in the course of the year (XLIII, 441). "Vous me comblez de joie en me faisant espérer que vous ne vous en tiendrez pas aux jésuites," exclaims Voltaire (XLIII, 457), and, as if to encourage his disciple in his resolution, he writes a week later: "Dieu vous maintienne, mon cher destructeur, dans la noble résolution où vous êtes de faire main basse sur les fanatiques, en faisant patte de velours!" (XLIII, 592). The failure of the Jansenists to arouse the Parlement against the *Destruction* gave a further impetus to d'Alembert's resolve, and he seems prepared to set

aside all restraint as he tells his master of their frustration:
"J'ai commencé par des croquignoles, je continuerai par les
coups de houssine, ensuite viendront les coups de gaule, et
je finirai par les coups de bâton; quand ils en seront là,
ils seront si accoutumés à être battus qu'ils prendront les
coups de bâton pour des douceurs. Mon Dieu, l'odieuse et
plate canaille! mais elle n'a pas longtemps à vivre, et je ne
lui épargnerai pas un coup de stylet" (XLIII, 545–46).[16]

This confident attitude was to be short-lived. The death
of Clairaut in May, 1765, had left his pension at the Académie des Sciences free for his successor, d'Alembert. The
confirmation by the government of the academy's request
that the pension be granted to d'Alembert should have been
a routine matter. But when, after a month's silence, the
appointment was still not forthcoming, it was obvious that
something was amiss. Voltaire tried to reassure his friend by
telling him that, since the pension had not been given to
anyone else, "on vous fait attendre: on veut peut-être que
vous fassiez quelque démarche" (XLIV, 8). It is true that
the minister, Saint-Florentin, has not given a definite answer on the pension, replies d'Alembert, but to make one
wait and to force him to go after what is justly his is almost
as great an outrage as to refuse him. The geometer then
complains of his poverty, the pension from the king of
Prussia being his main income, and he suggests that he
would leave France if he were not so old. The minister had
told Louis de Rohan that he had nothing against d'Alem-

16. For d'Alembert, the Jesuits, whom he called "les grenadiers
du Saint-Siège" (D'Al., V, 283), had been the real enemy and he did
not share Voltaire's fear that the Jansenists, having once destroyed
them, would turn on the Philosophes. He reassures the patriarch, declaring: "Le plus difficile sera fait quand la philosophie sera délivrée
des grands grenadiers du fanatisme et de l'intolérance; les autres ne
sont que des cosaques et des pandours qui ne tiendront pas contre nos
troupes réglées" (XLIII, 147). This attitude explains in part d'Alembert's willingness to let down his guard at this time.

bert, yet he was withholding his approval. The academician concludes by saying he has written the minister a letter which is neither fawning nor insolent and has received no reply. "Si on attend que je fasse d'autres démarches," he concludes, "on attendra longtemps" (XLIV, 12–13).

It seems clear that d'Alembert's independent and disdainful attitude toward "les puissances," which had long before been expressed in his *Essai sur la société des gens de lettres et des grands* (1753), may have had something to do with the apparent attempt to force him into a more tractable position. This, at any rate, is a possibility suggested by Voltaire. In a letter dated 8 July 1765 he tells his friend that the authorities know his unfavorable attitude toward those high up in the government because his letters have been opened at the post office. Seizing the opportunity to reinforce his argument for seeking protectors at the court, Voltaire then refers to the influence of the duc de Choiseul, suggesting that he may be the cause of Saint-Florentin's silence. Choiseul is still angry over the publication of *La Vision*, he confides, but he would like nothing better than to be d'Alembert's friend if only the latter were more complaisant. If d'Alembert would give him permission to write Choiseul, he is sure that the minister would give his approval (XLIV, 20). As might have been expected, d'Alembert belittled Choiseul's influence in the affair and blamed the "dévots de la cour" for the delay in his pension (XLIV, 27), thus forcing Voltaire to abandon his project of writing to the minister (XLIV, 37). The geometer shows his pleasure at his friend's decision by declaring: "Quoique je sens les inconvénients de la pauvreté, j'aime mieux rester pauvre que de devoir ma fortune à de pareilles gens" (XLIV, 40).

Despite his reiteration that the "cabale des dévots" is to blame for the delay, d'Alembert gives credence to Voltaire's theory that the ministers wanted to "cut him down to size" by admitting that Saint-Florentin may be hostile: "Ajoutez que ce petit bout de ministre, qui ne me voit jamais dans son antichambre avec mes autres confrères, a été tout capable de me prendre, pour cela seul, en aversion, et de chercher à me donner un dégoût qu'il n'ose pourtant consommer" (XLIV, 40). If the ministers Choiseul and Saint-Florentin had indeed sought to punish d'Alembert for his haughty and independent attitude by forcing him to beg for his pension, the plan backfired because public opinion was overwhelmingly in d'Alembert's favor, all the more so because he was seriously ill at the time.[17] He reveals his pleasure at this development by telling Voltaire that, since Paris has so well avenged him against Versailles, he has decided not to accept Frederick's invitation and has abandoned plans to leave France. He never expected such public support, he admits, and, since his difficulties have revealed to him that he has both prestige and friends, concludes that "it's an ill wind that blows no good" (XLIV, 41).

17. Apparently, rumor had it that the refusal of the pension had caused d'Alembert's illness. He denied this in a letter to the *Journal encyclopédique* dated 27 October 1765 in which he defended his right to the pension because of his seniority in the Académie des Sciences. Not everyone was convinced of the seriousness of d'Alembert's illness, as Bachaumont's discussion of the geometer's letter reveals: "Il prétend ensuite que sa maladie n'est point une suite du chagrin prétendu que le refus ou le délai de cette Pension lui ait causé; il joue la mauvaise santé et singe Voltaire en cette partie: il fait encore un étalage de sa Philosophie, et à travers de sa modestie on découvre l'orgueil le plus cynique, dont il a donné déjà trop de preuves." *Mémoires secrets*, II, 274. The refusal by d'Alembert of Frederick's invitation helped make a good impression on the public. When the geometer finally receives the pension, Bachaumont quotes the announcement from the *Journal encyclopédique* of 15 December 1765 which comments: "Ceux qui connaissent d'Alembert, ne s'étonneront pas qu'il ait fait à sa Patrie et à ses amis ce nouveau sacrifice. Il y aurait eu lieu de s'étonner que la France fût le seul pays où l'on ne rendît pas justice à un Savant qui donne de tels exemples." Ibid., pp. 308–9.

It appeared that d'Alembert was going to obtain his pension in spite of ministerial opposition. This was direct disproof of Voltaire's contention that the protection of nobles was necessary if the Philosophes were to succeed. D'Alembert cannot help rebuking his friend once more, in his conclusion to the letter to Voltaire, for the latter's policy of currying favor with certain noblemen: "Je suis fâché de vous l'avouer, mon cher et illustre maître; mais pourquoi n'épancherais-je pas mon cœur avec vous? vous avez un peu gâté les gens qui nous persécutent. J'avoue que vous avez eu besoin plus qu'un autre de les ménager, et que vous avez été obligé d'offrir une chandelle à Lucifer pour vous sauver de Belzébuth; mais Lucifer en est devenu plus orgueilleux, sans que Belzébuth en ait été moins méchant" (XLIV, 41). We could not expect Voltaire to pass over this statement in silence; but in both d'Alembert's accusation and in his correspondent's reply we note the absence of vehemence and emphatic declarations which typify their earlier letters on this subject. While maintaining their opinions, they seem more solicitous of their mutual friendship than of convincing each other. Thus d'Alembert now concedes that his master was obliged to show deference toward his noble friends, while Voltaire replies that his disciple is too just to expect him to break with those to whom he is greatly indebted. "Faut-il manquer à un homme qui nous a fait du bien, parce qu'il est grand seigneur?" he asks, and he concludes: "Je suis bien sûr que vous approuverez qu'on estime ou qu'on méprise, qu'on aime ou qu'on haïsse, très indépendamment des titres. Je vous aimerais, je vous louerais, fussiez-vous pape; et, tel que vous êtes, je vous préfère à tous les papes, ce qui n'est pas coucher gros; mais je vous aime et vous révère plus que personne au monde" (XLIV, 51–52).

There is evidence to indicate that d'Alembert's analysis of the situation was accurate and that his difficulties over his pension were due less to the personal resentment of the ministers than to the displeasure of the "dévots" over his *Destruction*. D'Alembert himself admits: "Je crois que la cabale des dévots, dont le petit bout de ministre Saint-Florentin a eu peur, y a eu plus de part que lui" (XLIV, 40). When the Académie des Sciences sent representatives to Saint-Florentin to inquire why the pension for d'Alembert was not forthcoming, Bachaumont relates, "le Ministre a répondu aux Députés de cette Compagnie que S. M. était trop mécontente des derniers ouvrages de M. d'Alembert pour lui accorder aucune grâce. On croit que ce discours tombe sur le livre concernant *la destruction des Jésuites*."[18] On 22 November 1765 d'Alembert announces to Voltaire that he has finally received his pension, but he has lost the enthusiasm for writing polemic brochures which he had developed after the success of his *Destruction*. Reflecting the same attitude of withdrawal from polemics he had developed in 1758 after his difficulties with his article "Genève," the geometer expresses his yearning to be wealthy enough to retire into the country and devote himself to study. He has written a supplement to the *Destruction*, he admits, but he does not know when, where or how he can publish it. And he reveals his bitterness by concluding: "Je voudrais bien servir la raison, mais je désire encore plus d'être tranquille. Les hommes ne valent pas la peine qu'on prend pour les éclairer; et ceux même qui pensent comme nous nous persécutent" (XLIV, 116).[19]

The years of debate over the two fundamental differences

18. Ibid., p. 214.

19. This last remark of d'Alembert is explained clearly by Pomeau, who in discussing the duc de Choiseul states: "Dans le cercle du premier ministre, le scepticisme mondain domine. On méprise les prêtres et la religion; mais on méprise autant les encyclopédistes, petits pédants qui n'ont pas les bonnes manières. La campagne contre l'infâme offense le bon ton. Entre le parti dévot et les philosophes, la politique de Choiseul louvoie avec une lassitude distinguée." *La Religion*, p. 332.

between Voltaire and d'Alembert had apparently done little toward resolving them. Despite the promise the *Destruction* had given of d'Alembert's change of attitude toward publication of controversial material, the resulting difficulties he had encountered had dampened his ardor. They had done more; they had embittered him all the more against Voltaire's protectors, the duc de Choiseul's circle, and had made impossible any conciliation on this point. When he had finally received his pension despite ministerial opposition, d'Alembert declared: "Vous croyez bien que je n'oublierai de ma vie cet outrage atroce et absurde" (XLIV, 115). He would not allow Voltaire to forget it either. Whether the patriarch took d'Alembert's statement, "et ceux même qui pensent comme nous nous persécutent," to mean Choiseul, or whether in answer to a nonextant letter from his disciple, Voltaire insisted that the minister had actually solicited the geometer's pension for him (XLIV, 189). D'Alembert replied: "Je ne sais pas si le ministre dont vous parlez est tel que vous dites; ce que je sais, c'est qu'à la mort de Clairaut, il a mieux aimé partager entre deux ou trois polissons une pension que Clairaut avait sur la marine que de me la donner . . . ce qui prouve, comme on dit, 'la bonne amitié des gens' " (XLIV, 238). It was futile to insist, and Voltaire merely expressed regret that Choiseul did not give him his just due, adding: "Je crois qu'il avait grand envie de se racommoder avec vous; mais vous n'êtes pas homme à faire les avances" (XLIV, 241–42). The stalemated debate over Choiseul was virtually abandoned after this exchange except for occasional but brief encounters.[20]

The fruitlessness of Voltaire's efforts to win over his

20. A translation of Tacitus in 1769 by La Blettrie containing notes insulting to the Philosophes was the occasion for a renewal of the debate. When the duc de Choiseul wrote Voltaire to defend La Blettrie, d'Alembert reiterated his anti-Choiseul position (the letter is not extant). Voltaire retorted: "Pardieu vous êtes bien injuste de

disciple to his way of thinking on this point led him to return to the second of their differences and try once again to
arouse him to a more active participation in the struggle
against "l'Infâme." The visit of Damilaville to Ferney in
August, 1765, which lasted until October of the same year,
served to reopen the question. During his stay, Damilaville
and his host made plans to produce various works for the
cause and to distribute them clandestinely in Paris. Voltaire
tells d'Alembert about the plan in a letter dated 16 October
1765. The brochures will be published under the name of
the deceased Boulanger, he explains, and he asks his disciple
to send him his contributions through Damilaville, admon-
ishing: "Vous êtes comptable de votre temps à la raison
humaine. Ayez l''inf———' en exécration, et aimez-moi"
(XLIV, 88).

---

me reprocher des ménagements pour gens puissants [sic], que je
n'ai connus jadis que pour gens aimables à qui j'ai les dernières obligations, et qui même m'ont défendu contre les monstres. En quoi
puis-je me plaindre d'eux?" (XLVI, 233). D'Alembert avoided a direct
reference to the question, but made a vague remark about "le despotisme ministériel" (XLVI, 237), to which Voltaire replied: "Je suis
devenu bien vieux et bien infirme; mais sachez que mes derniers jours
seraient persécutés sans la personne à qui je ne puis reprocher autre
chose, sinon de m'avoir assuré que La Blettrie n'avait pas pensé à moi"
(XLVI, 287–88). A year later d'Alembert complained of the praise
for Choiseul in Voltaire's *Questions sur l'"Encyclopédie"* (XLVII,
14). "Vous avez toujours sur le bout du nez un certain homme," countered Voltaire (XLVII, 24); to which his disciple replied that Choiseul
hates philosophy and letters, adding, by way of conciliation, that the
minister does have some praiseworthy qualities. The criticism was
not against the praise, but against placing it on the first page under
the letter "A" of the *Dictionnaire* (XLVII, 32). This was the last reference made by d'Alembert concerning Choiseul except to say in 1773
that the minister was contributing to the fund for Voltaire's statue
(XLVII, 92). This remark furnished the patriarch another opening
to defend his friend; he informs d'Alembert that Choiseul is protecting his watch-manufacturing establishment and has even helped him
sell some watches to the king (XLVII, 114, 130).

Capitulation

FOUR

IF D'ALEMBERT had been unable to budge the master from his position concerning the need for protectors at court, an event occurring in 1766 was to have a profound influence on Voltaire and bring him closer to his disciple's viewpoint regarding the polemic activities of "les frères." Although repressive measures had been taken from time to time against various Philosophes for their writings, Voltaire had retained his conviction that the opposition would be impotent to ward off a concerted attack. When in 1762 the Calas mon cher maître, de ne nous laisser égorger ni par personne incident had prompted d'Alembert to write: "Tâchons, ni pour personne" (XLII, 82), Voltaire had replied: "Que vous êtes tièdes à Paris" (XLII, 168). He had rejected his disciple's plea for an evolutionary approach and had even considered grooming Helvétius as a more outspoken Paris representative. D'Alembert's difficulties in obtaining his pension as a result of the publication of his *Sur la destruction des jésuites* had been an ineffective argument for the geometer's position. Indeed, the patriarch, spurred on by Damilaville's visit, seems to forget it completely and renews his efforts to get d'Alembert to take up arms again. A

more decisive argument against Voltaire's position was soon
to present itself, however, in the form of the execution of
the chevalier de la Barre in February, 1766.[1]

One week before hearing of the condemnation, Voltaire,
buoyed up by the recent visit of abbé Morellet, was in a
highly optimistic mood. In a letter dated 26 June 1766 he
tells d'Alembert of Morellet's visit and seeks to inspire him
with a missionary zeal for the cause: "L'Eglise de la sagesse
commence à s'étendre dans nos quartiers," he begins, "où
régnait, il y a douze ans, le plus sombre fanatisme. Les
provinces s'éclairent, les jeunes magistrats pensent haute-
ment; il y a des avocats généraux qui sont des anti-Omer."
After mentioning the enemies of the cause and the need to
attack them, he concludes with the familiar exhortation:
"Si vous n'écrasez pas l''inf . . . ,' vous avez manqué votre
vocation" (XLIV, 319).

Just five days later Voltaire, alarmed at the news of the
La Barre condemnation, asks d'Alembert to investigate the
matter for him (XLIV, 323), and on 7 July he writes abbé
Morellet to tell him the Philosophes have been accused in
the Parlement of having fomented the disrespectful actions
of La Barre and his friends through their writings. What is
most lamentable, he complains, is that these imputations
will be heard by the king and they will appear to be dictated
by patriotism and impartiality. In words reminiscent of
d'Alembert, he counsels Morellet: "Les philosophes doivent
toujours soutenir que tout philosophe qui est en vie est un

---

1. La Barre and four other young men had been accused of muti-
lating a crucifix, singing blasphemous songs, and failing to remove
their hats before the Blessed Sacrament during a procession. La Barre
and d'Etallonde were sentenced to have their tongues and hands cut
off and then to be burned. Voltaire immediately wrote a *Relation de
la mort du Chevalier La Barre* and later obtained a post in the army
of Frederick II for the fugitive d'Etallonde.

bon chrétien, un bon catholique." In the face of these serious accusations, he concludes, the "sages" must remain silent and wait (XLIV, 330). As usual with Voltaire, this momentary withdrawal in the face of danger was soon to be followed by a more vigorous approach: a week later he sends his *Relation de la mort du chevalier La Barre* to Damilaville. His fears for the flock in Paris were unabated, however, and the indifference of the public only made their danger more serious. Referring to the La Barre affair, Voltaire complains to d'Alembert that after talking about it briefly people flock to the Opéra-Comique and forget about it, "et la barbarie, devenue plus insolente par notre silence, égorgera demain qui elle voudra juridiquement; et vous surtout, qui aurez élevé la voix contre elle deux ou trois minutes" (XLIV, 347).

At the height of his anxiety, Voltaire already envisioned the destruction of the Philosophes. If they could not safely express their views in France, there was only one thing to do: leave the country. He then made a strong attempt to convince his friends in Paris of the necessity of going to Clèves, in Prussia, to form a colony of Philosophes where they could publish their writings unmolested (XLIV, 352, 356, 357, 358, 361, 366, 368, 375). The response was anything but encouraging. When Diderot failed to reply to his letter, Voltaire tried a further appeal through their mutual friend Damilaville (XLIV, 389–90). When Diderot finally did reply, it was to reinforce the position that d'Alembert had been maintaining all along: "Si nous ne concourons pas avec vous à écraser la bête, c'est que nous sommes sous sa griffe" (XLIV, 371). Voltaire expresses his disappointment at Diderot's refusal to leave Paris in a letter to Damilaville dated 25 August, wherein he complains that d'Alembert "m'ouvre son cœur, et M. Diderot me ferme le sien," and expresses his disgust at the inability of the brothers to unite:

"Je vois que les philosophes seront toujours de malheureux êtres isolés qu'on dévorera les uns après les autres, sans qu'ils s'unissent pour se secourir. 'Sauve qui peut!' sera la devise du commun naufrage" (XLIV, 398).[2]

The failure of Voltaire's plan to unite the Philosophes in a colony at Clèves had a twofold result. It underlined the fact that, of all his Paris friends, and in spite of their differences, d'Alembert still offered the chief hope of forming a united party. This became even more true with the death in 1768 of Damilaville, "l'intime ami de tous les Philosophes" (XLII, 37), who served as Voltaire's main link with Diderot and his disciples. It further underlined the futility of insisting on a polemic output patterned after his own and the necessity of following the geometer's plan of campaign. From this time on, Voltaire becomes more interested in d'Alembert's activities at the Académie française, and in seeing "le troupeau" grow in number and prestige under the watchful eye of his lieutenant.[3] D'Alembert, for his part,

2. Despite the disappointment of Diderot's refusal, Voltaire continued to hope for at least a visit from "Platon," as he called him. Writing to Damilaville on 10 September he exclaims: "O que je voudrais, mon cher ami, vous tenir avec Tonpla!" (XLIV, 421) And five days later: "Pourquoi M. Tonpla ne ferait-il pas ce petit voyage?" (XLIV, 429). Finally on 16 September he writes: "Je me porte fort mal, et je serai très fâché de mourir sans avoir vu Tonpla" (XLIV, 432). He was not to get his wish until his visit to Paris in 1778.

3. On 27 October 1766, for example, he suggests Thomas for the seat vacated by Hardion (D'Alembert, *Œuvres inéd.*, ed. Henry, p. 317), and two months later he asks d'Alembert to read La Harpe's *Discours des malheurs de la guerre* to the Académie to afford it a better chance to win the prize (XLIV, 547). When Thomas is accepted into the Académie, Voltaire writes d'Alembert: "Fourrez-moi beaucoup de ces gens-là dans l'Académie quand vous en trouverez" (XLV, 55). The following year he reminds d'Alembert that Chabanon and La Harpe should be groomed for entry into the Académie (XLV, 390). When Abbé d'Olivet dies in October, 1768, the patriarch inquires as to the choice of a successor to his academic seat (XLVI, 137). In June,

becomes more self-assured in his advice to his master and in his requests for brochures against their enemies.

The abandonment of the disagreement on the rôle of "les puissances," and the final acceptance by Voltaire of d'Alembert's conception of their respective rôles in the struggle, had the effect of eliminating a certain tension in the correspondence between the two Philosophes. A more affectionate note is discernible, as, for example, in Voltaire's statement: "Mon cher philosophe, vous êtes mon philosophe; plus je vous lis, plus je vous aime."[4] D'Alembert, too, seems to write with more warmth, even when he is reiterating his basic contention:

Je n'ai pas besoin de vous dire, ou plutôt de vous répéter, mon cher et illustre maître, avec quel plaisir j'ai lu ou plutôt relu ce que vous avez bien voulu m'envoyer; vous connaissez mon avidité pour tout ce qui vient de vous, et il ne tiendrait qu'à vous de la satisfaire encore mieux que vous ne faites. Je suis presque fâché quand j'apprends, par le public, que vous avez donné, sans m'en rien dire, quelque nouveau camouflet au fanatisme et à la tyrannie. . . . Il n'appartient qu'à vous de rendre ces deux fléaux du genre humain odieux et ridicules. Les honnêtes gens vous en ont d'autant plus d'obligation qu'on ne peut plus attaquer ces deux monstres que de loin. [XLV, 313]

This time Voltaire does not counter with an accusation of lukewarmness as he had so often done in the past, but concurs in his disciple's analysis of the situation by urging

1769, he writes: "Il faudrait que Marin fût un jour de l'Académie, et qu'il succédât à quelque cuistre à rabat pour purifier la place" (XLVI, 347). These are presented as examples: a complete list of references to the Académie française made by Voltaire would result in an unnecessary catalogue. In addition to his polemics, the patriarch was also busy with his manufacturing and farming activities at Ferney, and with his campaigns to defend Sirven and Martin from miscarriages of justice.

4. *Œuvres inéd.*, ed. Henry, p. 317. See also p. 314.

him to carry on the struggle by word of mouth since it is now impossible to print anything in Paris (XLV, 365). It was precisely in this type of action that d'Alembert had been engaged. One means utilized by the geometer for furthering the Philosophe cause was to point out to his fellow-country-men the high regard such enlightened greats as Frederick of Prussia had for his party. Thus, when the monarch had decried the brutality of the La Barre condemnation in a letter to d'Alembert, the latter had made its contents known in the Paris salons and then informed Frederick of the fact (D'Al., V, 266).

We have seen that on previous occasions Voltaire at times seems to concur in d'Alembert's views in one letter only to return to his vibrant appeal to "ecr. l'Inf——" in the next one. The extent of his capitulation to d'Alembert's point of view following the La Barre affair and the failure of his Clèves project can be measured in part by the conspicuous absence of this familiar call to arms in his letters from this time onward.[5] When he had first heard the news of La Barre's condemnation he had exclaimed: "Je ne vous dirai pas aujourd'hui, mon cher frère: 'Ecr. l'in——,' car c'est l''inf——' qui nous 'écr.'" (XLIV, 390). On 30 October 1767 he asks Damilaville why he does not publish his ob-servations on *L'Ordre essentiel des sociétés,* and, as if an-swering his own question he notes: "Mais il n'y a pas moyen de dire tout ce qu'on devrait et qu'on voudrait dire" (XLV, 421). Four days later he writes a pessimistic letter to d'Alem-bert reviewing the repressive measures taken against "les gens de lettres," culminating with the La Barre execution, and laments the inability of the Philosophes to write what

5. It does appear once in January, 1768, at the end of a letter to Damilaville, but it is qualified by: ". . . quand vous serez à la tête des vingtièmes" (XLV, 481). Five days later it is faintly suggested in an admonition to Marmontel: ". . . écrasez le monstre tout douce-ment" (XLV, 491), but these are its dying gasps: the era of "écrasez l'Infâme" was ended.

they think. But he urges his friend to continue working toward enlightenment at least verbally: "Vous ne voulez pas être martyr, mais soyez confesseur: vos paroles feront plus d'effet qu'un bûcher. Mon cher philosophe, criez toujours comme un diable" (XLV, 425). As we have seen, the spreading of the "gospel" by word of mouth was basically d'Alembert's method. When, the following month, the master tells his disciple: "Encore une fois, c'est l'opinion qui gouverne le monde, et c'est à vous de gouverner l'opinion" (XLV, 469), he again reflects his lieutenant's idea of winning the support of public opinion rather than of those in political power. The proximity of Voltaire's new outlook to that recommended by d'Alembert is even more marked when we recall the latter's previous statements concerning the spreading of tolerance while pretending to accept existing ideas, and when we read Voltaire's letter of May 1, 1768 to his disciple: "L'abominable jansénisme triomphe dans notre ridicule nation, et on ne détruit des rats que pour nourrir des crocodiles. A votre avis, que doivent faire les sages, quand ils sont environnés d'insensés barbares? il y a des temps où il faut imiter leurs contorsions, et parler leur langage" (XLVI, 36).

As if to put this principle into effect, Voltaire receives communion at Easter in April, 1768, while joking about it to d'Alembert (XLVI, 31, 36). Despite a preliminary acquiescence (XLVI, 41–42), the latter was displeased with the patriarch's communion. It was one thing for the Philosophes in Paris to be forced to pretend to have orthodox opinions,[6] but Voltaire, in d'Alembert's view, was supposed to vindicate them by defending them with his pen from his

6. Immediately after the La Barre incident d'Alembert wrote to Frederick: "Je crois, sire, que le seul parti à prendre pour un philosophe que sa situation empêche de s'expatrier, est de céder en partie à cet abominable torrent; de ne dire que le quart de la vérité, s'il y a trop de danger à la dire toute entière; ce quart sera toujours dit, et fructifiera sans nuire à l'auteur" (D'Al., V, 264).

vantage point of safety. Apparently d'Alembert was not the
only one to hold this view, because in a letter in which he
speaks "à cœur ouvert" he refers to Voltaire's complaint that
his friends have condemned his action openly. Some may
have done so, he concedes, but he was not among them although he disapproves of the communion as much as they.
The "dévots" will not be fooled by it, he pursues, and rather
than gain anything by it Voltaire may have placed himself
in grave danger by thus leaving himself open to accusations
of profanation of the sacrament. This is said in strictest con-
fidence, adds the geometer, and he has not spoken to anyone
else so frankly. He then concludes with a reiteration of his
devotion in terms which illustrate the point to which their
friendship has grown: "Quand vous feriez vos pâques tous
les jours, je ne vous en serais pas moins attaché comme au
soutien de la philosophie et à l'honneur des lettres. Sur ce,
je vous demand votre bénédiction, et surtout votre amitié,
en vous embrassant de tout mon cœur" (XLVI, 53).

Voltaire's fear of the power of his enemies at this time
seems to have outweighed the disapproval of his friends,
and the following year, after a repetition of his previous
Easter performance,[7] he wrote to d'Alembert to explain his
action. The bishop of Annecy, after writing against Vol-

7. When writing to Frederick in April, 1769, about the election
of a new pope for "la barque de S. Pierre," d'Alembert adds: "Voltaire me paraît un requin qui fait tout ce qu'il peut pour la renverser.
On dit pourtant qu'il voulait encore cette année-ci manger son Dieu
comme la précédente; mais on dit que son curé n'a pas voulu même
l'entendre en confession" (D'Al., V, 282). The "curé" of Ferney had
refused to bring him communion and the last rites unless he retracted
his irreligious works. After issuing a notarized declaration of adherence
to the Catholic faith, Voltaire received the last sacraments, explaining
his action to d'Argental as a necessity in "un diocèse ultramontain.
. . . je ne vois pas qu'il faille se faire regarder comme un monstre par
les barbares au milieu desquels je suis, pour un mince déjeuner:
c'est d'ailleurs un devoir de citoyen; le mépris marqué de ce devoir
aurait entraîné des suites désagréables pour ma famille" (XLVI, 308).

taire to the king, had recently caused a papal brief to be issued against him, "de sorte que je fus à la fois exposé à une lettre de cachet et à une excommunication majeure; . . . mais n'ayant pas la vocation du martyre, j'ai pris le parti de m'en tenir au rôle de confesseur, après avoir été fort singulièrement confessé" (XLVI, 336). Eleven days later he repeats his reasons for receiving communion and concludes: "En un mot on ne me traitera pas comme le chevalier de La Barre" (XLVI, 347).[8]

Voltaire's alarm is understandable when we consider the impact that the La Barre incident had on his outlook. When the Parlement of Toulouse had condemned the Protestant Calas family four years earlier, he had viewed it as a last trace of barbarism still existing in the provinces but certainly no longer possible at the capital. The La Barre condemnation, however, approved as it was not only by the Parlement of Paris but by the king himself, was all the more shocking for the ease with which the condemnation had been effected. If a teen-ager could be so easily executed for such a slight youthful imprudence, what could the Philosophes expect, whose writings had been blamed for leading the boys to their irreverent actions? It is true that d'Alembert tried to convince his friend that public opinion had reacted strongly against the judges responsible for the condemnation (XLIV, 403, 421), but the fact that Pasquier, who had engineered the judgment, was quoted as saying "qu'il ne fallait pas s'amuser à brûler des livres, que c'était les auteurs que Dieu demandait en sacrifice" (XLIV, 421), was certainly not reassuring.

Since Voltaire's convictions often became obsessions, it is

8. Pomeau is of the opinion that while Voltaire's communion in 1768 was motivated by "la crainte" (p. 436), the second, in 1769, was done "pour faire enrager son évêque" who had forbidden a repetition of the act (p. 437). The letter to d'Alembert, as well as that to d'Argental in footnote 7, suggests that fear of persecution was the motivating factor on both occasions.

not surprising to see him abandon the extreme optimism he exuded during his "écrasez l'Infâme" campaign for a mood of abject pessimism and an exaggerated view of the power of his opposition after the La Barre affair. So much did his bitterness permeate his writing during this period that d'Alembert found it necessary to calm his friend's alarms over the attacks made against him. Expressing surprise that the patriarch underestimates his own strength, he chides him for answering every "cuistre de collège" who mentions him, thus giving them an existence. More important, Voltaire's latest brochure, the *Réponse à Warburton,* is too bitter in tone: he should attack more gaily. "Vous êtes si persuadé," he adds, "qu'il faut rire de tout, et vous savez si bien rire quand vous voulez; que ne riez-vous donc toujours, puisque Dieu vous a fait la grâce de le pouvoir?" And he concludes: "Portez-vous bien, et surtout riez" (XLV, 333–34).[9] On another occasion Voltaire decries the power of the Jansenists since the destruction of the Jesuits. He reminds d'Alembert of his prediction that they had been delivered from the foxes only to be abandoned to the wolves, and complains: "Les honnêtes gens ne peuvent combattre qu'en se cachant derrière les haies" (XLV, 331–32).

9. D'Alembert rightly recognized Voltaire's scathing wit as one of his most effective weapons. The complete discrediting of Lefranc de Pompignan following his anti-Philosophe speech in the Académie française had been ample proof of this; therefore, when the patriarch did not make full use of this talent, or when he stooped to the adulation of "les puissances," d'Alembert could judge the master quite severely. In July, 1763, for example, during his sojourn in Prussia, the geometer writes to his friend Mlle de Lespinasse: "Ah! mon Dieu! oui, ce huitième volume de Voltaire [*Essai sur l'histoire générale*] est à faire vomir par la bassesse et la platitude de ses éloges. C'est bien la peine d'avoir plus de cent mille livres de rente et d'être dans un pays libre pour écrire ainsi l'histoire. Et à qui croit-il en imposer? Cela fait pitié. Il est bien digne après cela d'avoir fait une platte parodie de réquisitoire d'Omer qu'il était si aisé de tourner en ridicule." D'Alembert, *Œuvres inéd.,* ed. Henry, p. 292.

The geometer agrees, but counters Voltaire's excessive pessimism by adding: ". . . mais ils peuvent appliquer de là de bons coups de fusil contre les bêtes féroces qui infestent le pays" (XLV, 353). A few years earlier, the rôles might have been reversed. One has the impression that d'Alembert is attempting to bolster his friend's morale during this mood of depression and to prevent him from going to extremes in his attitude.

Voltaire's pessimism at this time is typical of his reaction in periods of difficulty. As early as his Colmar sojourn in 1753, when he was desperately seeking refuge from imminent persecution, he had been so depressed as to wish he were dead (Best., XXIII, 283). Yet he managed to fight off despair by immersing himself in his literary activity. When, the following year, he heard of the suicide of Deker, a Bâle bookseller, he remarked: "Il faut toujours l'objet d'une occupation, sans quoi je trouverais le parti de Deker fort raisonnable" (Best., XXIV, 28). So too after the La Barre affair, the polemic brochures pouring from the patriarch's pen served as an outlet for his frustrations and sustained his ardor for the Philosophe cause.[10] The chief modification in his attitude on that score was his insistence that his authorship be more carefully hidden than heretofore, and he asks d'Alembert and his friends to help in this endeavor (XLVI, 36).

In pointing to the circumstances leading to Voltaire's acceptance of d'Alembert's views and to his Easter communions in 1768 and 1769, there is the danger of painting only the sombre side the better to reinforce the point. Yet,

10. Among these works were *L'Ingénu, Profession de foi des théistes, Les Colimaçons du R. P. l'Escarbotier, Droit des hommes, Trois Empereurs,* a new edition of the *Siècle de Louis XIV* augmented by a *Siècle de Louis XV,* an *Histoire du Parlement, L'Anecdote sur "Bélisaire"; Les Honnêtetés littéraires, La Guerre de Genève, Les Questions de Zapata.* For a more complete listing see Pomeau's *La Religion,* pp. 348–50.

despite the bleakness of the situation, there were several
events which offered hope for the future and which served
to cheer the patriarch at this time. In the spring of 1767,
for example, d'Alembert, perhaps in part to bolster Voltaire's spirits, as well as to give vent to his own resentment
over the recent renewal of repressive tendencies in France,
sent to Voltaire his anti-Jansenist *Lettre à M. ——— conseiller
du parlement de ———*, which he had written in 1755 but had
withheld following the difficulties over his pension. In a
letter dated 3 May 1767 Voltaire expresses his pleasure and
asks hopefully: "Ne voudriez-vous point ajouter à l'histoire
de la *Destruction* quelque chose concernant l'Espagne?"
(XLV, 248). D'Alembert obliged ten days later with a
Seconde Lettre à M. ——— etc., sur l'édit du roi d'Espagne.[11]
A further encouragement for Voltaire which may also help
explain d'Alembert's release of his brochures at this time,
was the embarrassment and ridicule which the Sorbonne had
brought upon itself following its condemnation of thirty-
seven propositions from Marmontel's *Bélisaire.* The objec-

11. The king of Spain had suddenly decided to expel the Jesuits
from his domain but had refused to give any reasons, saying only that
they were "locked in his heart." He had further prohibited any writing in the Jesuits' defense. While pleased at their suppression, d'Alembert did not approve the king's methods, and he writes Voltaire:
"Mais que dites-vous de l'édit du roi d'Espagne, qui les chasse si
brusquement? Persuadé, comme moi, qu'il a eu pour cela de très
bonnes raisons, ne pensez-vous pas qu'il aurait bien fait de les dire,
et ne les pas renfermer 'dans son cœur royal'? Ne pensez-vous pas
qu'on devrait permettre aux jésuites de se justifier surtout quand on
doit être sûr qu'ils ne le peuvent pas? ne pensez-vous point encore
qu'il serait très injuste de les faire tous mourir de faim, si un seul
frère coupe-chou s'avise d'écrire bien ou mal en leur faveur?" (XLV,
250). The *Seconde Lettre . . . sur l'édit du roi d'Espagne* upholds the
king's action while regretting that his reasons were not made public,
and, after suggesting that all priests and monks are potential dangers
to the State, d'Alembert expresses the hope that other nations will follow Spain's example (D'Al., II, 109–17).

tion to such statements as: "La vérité luit par sa propre lumière, et on n'éclaire pas les esprits à la lueur des bûchers," left the Sorbonne open to attack not only from the Philosophes but from churchmen themselves. When the Sorbonne attempted to keep the list of condemned propositions from the public, writes d'Alembert to Voltaire, Marmontel's friends had it printed. And he concludes: "Je me flatte que le cri public va les faire rentrer dans la boue, et qu'ils n'oseront pas publier leur censure, tant la seule liste des propositions les rendra d'avance odieux et ridicules!" (XLV, 256–57). Shortly afterwards Turgot published *Les XXXVIII Vérités opposées aux XXXVII impiétés de "Bélisaire," par un bachelier ubiquiste.*

As might be expected, Voltaire could not resist entering the fray, and on 16 May 1767 he writes to Marmontel asking for particulars and offering to write a brochure ridiculing the Sorbonne (XLV, 265). The Marmontel-Sorbonne affair, together with d'Alembert's brochures, caused a surge of optimism in the patriarch. As in the case of the *Destruction*, he had taken charge of sending his disciple's *Seconde Lettre . . . sur l'édit du roi d'Espagne* to Cramer for publication. When he mails d'Alembert his copies he shows his exuberance by affirming that Europe is opening its eyes: "Bénissons cette heureuse révolution qui s'est faite dans l'esprit de tous les honnêtes gens depuis quinze ou vingt années; elle a passé mes espérances." As for "la canaille," he continues, he does not bother with them: "Je cultive mon jardin, mais il faut bien qu'il y ait des crapauds; ils n'empêchent pas mes rossignols de chanter. Adieu, aigle; donnez cent coups de bec aux chouettes qui sont encore dans Paris" (XLV, 284–85). This is certainly a joyful note, but Voltaire recognizes his own propensity to allow the latest event to affect his mood when he confides to Damilaville: ". . . tantôt je pleure, tantôt je ris" (XLV, 265).

D'Alembert, as we have seen, encouraged his friend to

laugh at his enemies and urged him to continue to mock
them in his brochures. But he also bolstered the master's
spirits by sending news of his own activities in furthering
the prestige of "le troupeau" through the Académie française, and by interesting foreign monarchs in the Philosophe
cause.[12] Thus when the king of Denmark visited the Académie des Sciences while in Paris in December, 1768,
d'Alembert took the opportunity to praise "philosophy" in
a speech before the monarch on that occasion, and he later
reported to Voltaire with satisfaction the favorable effect of
his oration on the king (XLVI, 194).[13] In addition to this
speech, d'Alembert had the opportunity to speak to the king
at greater length concerning Voltaire. He tells his friend
about it in a subsequent letter: "Il me parla beaucoup de
vous; des services que vos ouvrages avaient rendus, des
préjugés que vous avez détruits, des ennemis que votre
liberté de penser avait faits; vous vous doutez bien de mes
réponses" (XLVI, 183).

12. In 1771, when the royal prince of Sweden was declared king
on the death of his father, Bachaumont records the event and gives
us an insight into d'Alembert's success in gaining the favor of foreign
monarchs for his cause. After praising the new king, Bachaumont
notes: "Il a presque toujours été entouré des Philosophes Encyclopédistes; mais M. d'Alembert est celui qu'il a distingué le plus, et
qu'il a particulièrement admis à son intimité: tous s'accordent à le
regarder comme un sectateur zélé de leur doctrine, et se flattent de
trouver aujourd'hui un protecteur puissant dans ce nouveau Roi."
Mémoires, V, 263.

13. Bachaumont, knowing d'Alembert's aversion to adulating the
nobility, seems to admire the way the geometer acquitted himself on
this occasion. He writes: "M. d'Alembert, peu louangeur de son naturel, a fait un discours sur 'l'influence et l'utilité réciproques de la
Philosophie envers les Princes, et des Princes envers la Philosophie.'
Il a enchassé naturellement dans sa dissertation l'éloge du Roi présent,
et par cette tournure oratoire a évité ce que pouvait avoir de fade
un éloge direct dans la bouche d'un Encyclopédiste." Ibid., IV, 186.

D'Alembert seconded his cheerful reports by sending more pilgrims than ever to visit the master at Ferney. We find letters of recommendation from the geometer for Chabanon (XLV, 250), the marquis de Mora (XLVI, 28), the chamberlain to the king of Sweden, Mr. Jennings (XLVI, 236), the publisher Panckoucke (XLVII, 103), and the comte de Schombert (XLVI, 391). The visit of the last named had a particularly salutary effect on his host, who reports enthusiastically to d'Alembert that this "ange consolateur" is "un des plus aimables hommes du monde: vous me l'aviez bien dit, il y en a peu dans la milice céleste qui lui soit comparable" (XLVI, 390–91). But his joy is not without a tinge of regret that such good soldiers cannot fight more freely. No doubt recalling the aborted plan for a colony of Philosophes at Clèves, Voltaire concludes: "Il faudrait avoir établi une ville de philosophes comme Tycho-Brahé fonda Uranembourg. Par quelle fatalité est-il plus aisé de rassembler des laboureurs et des vignerons que des gens qui pensent! . . . Ma consolation est que vous m'aimiez un peu; moi je vous aime beaucoup, et de toutes mes forces" (XLVI, 391).

Voltaire was to be even further consoled by his friends when, the following year, at a dinner at the home of Mme Necker, d'Alembert and "les frères" decided to launch a subscription for funds to erect a statue to their leader. In a letter of introduction for the sculptor Pigalle, d'Alembert tells his friend that many have already contributed, including the duc de Richelieu, and the duc de Choiseul has promised to join the list (XLVII, 92). In his reply Voltaire enclosed a poem to those who frequented Mme Necker's salon to show his appreciation, and he tells d'Alembert: "C'est un beau soufflet, mon cher et vrai philosophe, que vous donnez au fanatisme et aux lâches valets de ces monstres. . . . Vous écrasez sous ce marbre la superstition, qui levait encore la tête" (XLVII, 116).[14] One bitter note in connection with the subscription was the sudden reappearance in Paris at this time of Jean-Jacques Rousseau, who, upon hearing of the proposed statue to Voltaire, chose to send a contribution. When d'Alembert told the patriarch about it (XLVII, 124), the latter was furious, and insisted the money be returned (XLVII, 140–41, 153), but the geometer reminded his master of the partisans of "ce charlatan" and of his own desire to avoid difficulties with them (XLVII, 162). The reminder of the strength of Rousseau's protectors as well as the desire to avoid exposing his friend to their attacks caused Voltaire to acquiesce reluctantly.[15]

Paradoxically, at the very moment that the Philosophes chose to present a semblance of solidarity by erecting a statue to their "leader," their movement had already split into two camps: the Voltaire-d'Alembert group, and the Diderot-d'Holbach faction. In 1770, precisely when d'Alembert was soliciting contributions for the monument to the author of *La Henriade,* the appearance of d'Holbach's *Système de la nature* brought the rift into the open and caused

14. The name of Choiseul on the list of subscribers gave Voltaire an opportunity to defend the nobleman once more. In his reply he affirms: ". . . soyez très certain que sans Palissot, fils de son avocat, et sans Fréron, qui a été son régent au collège des jésuites, il aurait été votre meilleur ami: je le crois actuellement revenu" (XLVII, 116). Details concerning the subscription for a statue to Voltaire are amply covered by Desnoiresterres (*Voltaire et la société,* VII, 332–50) and need not be reiterated here.

15. Rousseau's differences with Voltaire and with David Hume are frequently alluded to in the d'Alembert-Voltaire correspondence during this period (1760–70). D'Alembert's rôle in these quarrels has been more fully treated in my "Rousseau and d'Alembert." Details concerning the Voltaire-Rousseau quarrel can be had in George Havens' "Voltaire, Rousseau, and the *Lettre sur la Providence,*" *PMLA,* LIX (March, 1944), 109–30. Gaston Maugras, *Voltaire et Rousseau* (Paris, 1886) gives a more detailed account but is biased and less reliable.

Voltaire to exclaim: "Voilà une guerre civile entre les incrédules" (XLVII, 153). But he did not despair: he continued to believe that theirs was a common cause and that
conciliation was still possible. In announcing to d'Alembert
his refutation of d'Holbach's *Système* the patriarch laments:
"Nos ennemis diront que la discorde est dans le camp d'Ag-
ramant. Toutefois il faut que les deux partis se réunissent.
Je voudrais que vous fissiez cette reconciliation" (XLVII,
153).

As in his plan for a colony of Philosophes in Clèves, Voltaire, in his idealistic desire for union, failed to see the depth
of the cleavage between the two groups, nor was he aware
of the extent to which the Diderot-d'Holbach faction
scorned his own by then conservative position.[16] In order to
understand more fully the relative positions of the two
factions, as well as Voltaire's conviction that d'Alembert
alone could mediate the dispute, it might be well to broaden
our sights somewhat at this point and review the background of the "guerre civile" announced by Voltaire.

16. In discussing Voltaire's Clèves plan, Pomeau comments: "Bien
entendu, Diderot fait échouer ces beaux projets, en refusant de
quitter Paris. Il fallait être aussi piètre psychologue que Voltaire
pour s'y obstiner comme il fit." *La Religion,* p. 346.

Civil War

FIVE

I NASMUCH as church and state, in the eighteenth century, were intimately linked, it is not surprising that a clash within the Philosophe ranks would reflect a twofold aspect, the one metaphysical, the other political. The two are so interrelated that it would be difficult to treat them separately, however tempting the convenient categories might appear. I shall therefore attempt to consider at the same time the doctrinal differences between the Voltaire-d'Alembert and the Diderot-d'Holbach groups, and their views concerning the practical application of those doctrines to the state.

When, in 1747, La Mettrie set forth his atheistic views in *L'Homme machine*, his was considered an extreme, and even radical, position. Indeed, it had been the cause of his flight to the court of Frederick of Prussia. Diderot, just the year before, had expressed in his *Pensées philosophiques* a deistic philosophy which generally reflected that of Voltaire, but the seeds of materialism were also interspersed throughout his arguments.[1] When, however, two years later,

1. Torrey ("Voltaire's Reaction," pp. 1128–29) has published Vol-

81

Diderot published his *Lettre sur les aveugles* (1749) in which the blind man, Saunderson, presents arguments for atheism, Voltaire did not limit himself to marginal comments but pointed out his disapproval to the author (Best., XVII, 86–87). Diderot's reply that he did not share Saunderson's sentiments, and his remark, "Je crois en dieu, quoique je vive très bien avec les athées" (Best., XVII, 90, 92), may have pleased his correspondent, but the detailed arguments in favor of his atomic theory of the universe could not so easily be dismissed. Yet these were only theoretical considerations without immediate practical application, and, as such, were less important to Voltaire.

The appearance of La Mettrie's *Anti-Sénèque, ou le souverain bien* in 1750, however, caused Voltaire some alarm. Here La Mettrie was not merely indulging in metaphysical speculation but was applying his materialistic conclusions to social conduct: vices and virtue were merely political institutions; only fools felt remorse for their conduct; morality was not the basis of man's happiness; the only preoccupation for man was the satisfaction of his bodily needs. The

taire's marginal comments in the 1746 edition of the *Pensées philosophiques* showing the patriarch's concern with the arguments for a chance formation of the universe: "Vous supposez l'existence de ces dés—c'est clair que rafle de six doit arriver; mais la question est, s'il y a des dés: point de dés, point d'arrangements, point d'ordre sans intelligence. . . . Tout ouvrage prouve un ouvrier." Max Wartofsky, in his "Diderot and the Development of Materialist Monism," suggests that Diderot's deism in the *Pensées philosophiques* was "a disguised atheism for the benefit of the royal censor. . . ." *Diderot Studies*, ed. Otis Fellows and Norman Torrey, II (Syracuse, 1952), p. 328. Aram Vartanian's "From Deist to Atheist," on the other hand, presents Diderot's deism at this point as an early position later abandoned for atheism under the influence of the biological sciences. *Diderot Studies*, I (1949), 47–63. Given the searching character of Diderot's writings and the more solid documentation of the latter article, Vartanian's position appears to me more realistic.

atheists, since they participated in the struggle against "le fanatisme," could be tolerated for their metaphysical position (XLVI, 300), but this was going too far: "Il y a une grande différence entre combattre les superstitions des hommes et rompre les liens de la société et les chaînes de la vertu" (Best., XX, 188). For Voltaire, a belief in God and in fixed principles of right and wrong were essential to society, first as a curb for the monarch: "Un roi athée est plus dangereux qu'un Ravaillac fanatique" (XXI, 573); secondly, as a means of instilling virtue in the masses: "La croyance des peines et des récompenses après la mort est un frein dont le peuple a besoin" (XXVI, 511–12).

In his reply to La Mettrie's *Anti-Sénèque*, the *Poème sur la religion naturelle*, the stress which Voltaire places on eternal fixed principles of morality engraved by God in the hearts of all men, reveals his concern with the social consequences of La Mettrie's invitation to an unbridled self-indulgence. Nor does he stop at his reaffirmation of natural religion as a guide to men's conduct. He sets to work writing a refutation of atheism (the article "Athéisme" of the *Dictionnaire philosophique,* also published as *Athée I*). The detailed exposition and refutation of Diderot's theory of the chance creation of the universe through the interplay of constantly moving atoms from all eternity, as expounded in the *Pensées philosophiques,* show clearly that Voltaire, despite his silence before Diderot's arguments, had not forgotten the Encyclopedist's letter of three years earlier. It indicates too that Voltaire is not concerned only about La Mettrie; henceforth, he will look with growing uneasiness upon the entire nascent atheistic wing of the Encyclopedic party as represented by Diderot.[2]

2. Pomeau states: "La réaction de Voltaire, en 1752, par delà la coterie frédéricienne, désavoue les premières manifestations de ce qui sera la coterie holbachique." *La Religion,* p. 279.

The ensuing six years were to provide a lull in the disagreement. The editors of the *Encyclopédie* had obtained
several articles from Voltaire and the agreement on attacking their mutual enemies overshadowed any differences
which might have existed. But Diderot's intellectual odys-
sey from deism to atheism had not stopped for that. In 1749
he had secured the co-operation of baron d'Holbach for
many of the scientific articles in the *Encyclopédie*.[3] While
a traditional opinion exists that Diderot influenced his new
collaborator into accepting atheism,[4] it seems more accurate to consider d'Holbach's militant atheism as having
influenced the still vacillating Diderot.[5] However that may
be, Pierre Naville, in his *Paul Thiry d'Holbach* (p. 22), calls
their liaison "l'élément capital de la consolidation du noyau
encyclopédique." Certainly, Diderot's *Pensées sur l'inter-
prétation de la nature,* published in 1754, reflected a strong-
er commitment to atheistic materialism than had his earlier
works. It would be interesting to know why Voltaire seems
unaware of the publication of the *Pensées* until six years
later, when, after asking Thieriot and Damilaville for a

3. See notes in Roth, III, 326, 327.

4. D.-J. Garat in his *Mémoires historiques sur la vie de M. Suard,
sur ses écrits et sur le XVIIIᵉ siècle* (Paris, 1820), I, 208–9, recounts an
undocumented anecdote which pictures d'Holbach as a young believer attempting to sway Diderot from his atheism but falling on his
knees before the superior reasoning of the Encyclopedist to rise again
an atheist. See Virgil W. Topazio's *D'Holbach's Moral Philosophy*
(Genève, 1956), pp. 95–97, for a refutation of this version.

5. In discussing Garat's account mentioned above, Pierre Naville
states: "Tout prouve au contraire que d'Holbach était déjà en 1750,
matérialiste." *Paul Thiry d'Holbach et la philosophie scientifique au
XVIIIᵉ siècle* (Paris, 1943), p. 27. Topazio (p. 95) argues from this:
"It is logical to suppose that the scientifically-minded d'Holbach, at
whose home Diderot was spending a great deal of his time, contributed to the change in Diderot's thought from a sceptical deism to an
atheistic materialism."

copy (XL, 424, 438), he thanks the latter for the book on 19 March 1761 and expresses his intention to read it (XLI, 240).[6] It may be that d'Alembert, who was anxious to retain Voltaire's name for the encyclopedic enterprise, had thought it wiser to avoid sending Voltaire a book of which he would probably disapprove.

Voltaire's disagreement with Diderot's metaphysical views did not prevent him from desiring a closer harmony in pursuing their common cause. The appearance in 1758 of Helvétius' *De l'esprit*, and the ensuing persecution of the Encyclopedists with which it was linked,[7] increased his desire to be of service to the group. Despite his declaration that he was far from sharing the opinions of Helvétius (Best., XXXIV, 163), and his reproach to the author of *De l'esprit* for having placed friendship among the base passions (ibid., p. 244), the widespread condemnation of *De l'esprit*, the *Encyclopédie*, and his own *Poème sur la religion naturelle* on 6 February 1759 caused him to rally to their defense. Referring to Helvétius and Diderot, he tells Thieriot: "J'estime beaucoup ces deux hommes, et les indignités qu'ils éprouvent me les rendent infiniment chers" (Best., XXXV, 76). He then asks for the names of the enemies of the *Encyclopédie* and begins an active campaign in its defense.[8]

It seems evident, therefore, that despite his disagreement

6. He makes no further mention of the work and there are no marginal comments in the volume in his library at Leningrad. See Torrey, pp. 1135–36.

7. Barbier's *Journal* (VII, 79) notes the stir which *De l'esprit* has made in Paris and reports that it is considered to represent the theories of the Encyclopedists. See Roth, II, 64.

8. See Chapter I above. A more detailed account of Voltaire's defense of the *Encyclopédie* may be found in my *Berthier's Journal de Trévoux*, pp. 118–33. For more information on the relations between Voltaire and Helvétius see Keim, *Helvétius*, pp. 433–55.

with the atheistic doctrines of both Diderot and Helvétius,
Voltaire considered them brothers-in-arms and was willing
to overlook their metaphysical differences. Why then, beginning in 1760, did a serious rift become evident between
the two factions? The reason has already been suggested in
Chapter III, for it was the same cause which set d'Alembert
at odds with his master despite their mutual adherence to
a skeptical deism: Voltaire seemed too attached to "les
puissances." Not that Voltaire subscribed to the abuses of
the Bourbon reigns. As Henri Sée points out, his conception
of the state was fraught with revolutionary consequences
because he made the abuses of the Old Régime unbearable
to his contemporaries and demanded reforms which could
only come "le jour où s'effondrerait tout ce système politique et social. . . ."[9] But the Voltairian paradox is precisely
his setting forth of revolutionary ideas only to refuse to follow them to their logical consequences. Thus his *Lettres
philosophiques* (1734) had attacked the concept of the
spirituality and immortality of the soul by putting forth the
Lockean suggestion that thought could be simply another
property of matter. In his reply to Voltaire's letter criticizing
the blind Saunderson's atheism in his *Lettre sur les aveugles*
(1749), Diderot reminds his critic that the latter's position
is a further argument for atheism: "Quelle force n'ajou-
terait point à ce raisonnement l'opinion qui vous est commune avec Locke que la pensée pourrait bien être une modification de la matière" (Best., XVII, 91). Disregarding this
reminder, Voltaire persisted in upholding the same idea in
his *Micromégas* (1752), and in 1757 he writes to d'Alembert
concerning the *Encyclopédie*: "Je prie l'honnête homme

9. *L'Evolution de la pensée politique en France au XVIII⁰ siècle*
(Paris, 1925), p. 132. A recent study, *Voltaire and the State* (New York,
1955), by Constance Rowe, gives a sympathetic exposition of Voltaire's
struggle for political reforms. See also Peter Gay, *Voltaire's Politics:
the Poet as Realist* (Princeton, 1959).

qui fera 'Matière' de bien prouver que le je ne sais quoi
qu'on nomme 'matière' peut aussi bien penser que le je ne
sais quoi qu'on appelle 'esprit' " (Best., XXXI, 247).

To understand Voltaire's continued use of the argument
even though it seemed to reinforce an atheistic position,
we must, in the words of Lester G. Crocker, "look behind
the statement to the target."[10] In his efforts to discredit revealed religion in favor of natural religion, Voltaire had
found Locke's suggestion useful in undermining the doctrine of the immortality of the soul. One of Voltaire's sever-
est contemporary critics, the Jesuit journalist Berthier, had
pointed this out to his readers when reviewing the *Poème
sur la loi naturelle* in 1757: "Ce poème paraît destiné à ré-
futer l'athéisme; mais entraîné par ses préjugés et par son
zèle contre la religion révélée, l'auteur, en creusant les fondements du naturalisme se propose de saper ceux du Christianisme." That is why, pursues the critic, the author fur-
nishes arms to both the atheists and the theologians. Turning to Voltaire's rejection of the immortality of the soul and
his suggestion that matter can think, a position which the
journalist points out as the basis for materialism, he concludes: "Ainsi le Matérialisme vient de lui-même sur les
fondements que M. de V. a préparés pour le Naturalisme;
sans que ce Poète se soit réservé aucun moyen de l'exclure
de son système."[11] The accuracy of the evaluation seemed
borne out by Voltaire's own gradual acceptance, through
Malebranche and Spinoza, of a position closer to that of

10. "Voltaire's Struggle for Humanism," *Studies on Voltaire and
the Eighteenth Century* (Genève, 1957), IV, 142. Discussing the con-
tradictions in Voltaire's ideas, Crocker states (p. 165): "It is . . . his
habit of considering problems in terms of their practical or propa-
gandistic consequences, and his emotional peripeteia, that gives us
the most obvious explanation of his divergences."

11. *Mémoires pour l'histoire des sciences et beaux-arts* (April,
1757), II, 1088–89.

Diderot and his coterie. Yet here again he refused to take the final step and clung tenaciously to his concept of a supreme being.[12]

There is an element of nostalgic emotion in Voltaire's refusal to abandon the old aristocratic traditions he had lauded in his *Siècle de Louis XIV*, and in his loyalty to certain friends among the nobility, despite their unfriendliness or indifference toward the Philosophe movement. It is in part because of this refusal to abandon what they considered vestiges of a bygone age that the Holbachic group held the patriarch in suspicion. D'Alembert himself, as we have seen in the case of Choiseul and Mme du Deffand, was frequently annoyed at the master for his persistent refusal to break with his old friends even though they protected the enemies of the Philosophes. When he rebuked Voltaire for his friendship with the duc de Richelieu despite the latter's rôle in the defeat of Philosophe candidates for the Académie française, the patriarch apologized: "J'espère que vous me pardonnerez d'avoir respecté un ancien attachement" (XLVIII, 567). The same loyalty to the past explains his lingering affection for some of his Jesuit teachers despite his attacks on their order. As late as 1768, on the death of abbé d'Olivet, whom d'Alembert called "ce gros ex-jésuite" (D'Al., V, 271), Voltaire, in the face of his friend's animosity, wrote: "L'abbé d'Olivet est un bon homme, et je l'ai toujours aimé. D'ailleurs il a été mon préfet dans le temps qu'il y avait des jésuites. Savez-vous que j'ai vu passer le P. le Tellier et le P. Bourdaloue, moi qui vous parle?" (XLVI, 111). Such an attitude toward the past was considered by the Philosophes as a weakness and an evidence of lukewarmness toward the cause. Voltaire's vacillation in the affair over Palissot's *Philosophes* seemed the final proof that

12. See Torrey's "Voltaire's Reaction" for an exposition of Voltaire's final position and his attitude of "mystic adoration" toward the Creator. Pomeau (*La Religion,* pp. 410 ff.) concurs in Torrey's analysis.

in a showdown between "les puissances" and his own party, the patriarch's effectiveness would be cancelled out by his loyalty to those in power. It is in consequence of the Palissot affair that the Diderot-d'Holbach wing decided to fight the battle in its own way and under its own banner.[13]

Voltaire, as has been shown, had more valid reasons than mere nostalgia for not wishing to antagonize the ruling powers. His aim was not the overthrow of the monarchy but a general education of the ruling class in his liberal ideas. As he had so often told d'Alembert, reforms would have to come from the top. The real obstacle to a better life was not the monarchy but the church: if a wedge could be driven between church and state, and his own natural religion put in its place, the battle would be won.[14] D'Alembert, with some exceptions, was in basic agreement with Voltaire. We have seen his plan for a gradual, evolutionary spread of enlightenment. He believed in the ultimate success of his cause through a cautious dissemination of liberal ideas, but unlike Voltaire's plan, this was not to be achieved through the currying of favor with the rulers. It was to be forced on them through a public opinion molded by "men of letters." If enough great men in the realm shared his liberal views, and if they became widespread throughout Europe, France could not help but follow. Henri Sée, in his *Evolution de la pensée politique* (p. 123), states that

13. Pomeau (ibid., pp. 332–33) in speaking of Voltaire's caution in the Palissot affair states that "le clan de Diderot lui reproche de flatter bassement les puissances," and he continues: "En effet, depuis l'affaire Palissot, le clan encyclopédique ne veut pas recevoir l'évangile voltairien. Le jour est proche où la rue Royale-Saint-Roche entreprendra d'*écraser l'infâme*, par ses moyens propres, sans autrement s'occuper des travaux apostoliques de Ferney."

14. "L'infâme," states Pomeau, "c'est le christianisme" (ibid., p. 310). In overthrowing it, "il faut répéter aux têtes couronnées qu'ils ont dans les prêtres des ennemis, et dans les philosophes des alliés" (p. 315).

Voltaire would have been satisfied with constitutional guar-
antees and would have accepted an absolute ruler as long as
he guaranteed his subjects their natural rights. This could
be said equally well of d'Alembert, who writes: "Je pense
que la forme du gouvernement est indifférente en elle-
même, pourvu que le gouvernement soit juste, que tous les
citoyens aient également droit à sa protection, qu'ils soient
également soumis aux lois, et également punis s'ils les violent; que les supplices ne soient pas réservés pour les petits
coupables, et les honneurs pour les grands" (D'Al., V, 298).

Diderot and Voltaire, on the other hand, were poles apart
in their political views. Whereas d'Alembert and his master
would have settled for liberal reforms under an enlightened
monarch, Diderot was suspicious of any absolute monarch,
no matter how enlightened. In fact, a good king is even
more dangerous than a bad one because he accustoms his
people to serve his successor, however inept, without question: "Il enlève au peuple le droit de délibérer, de vouloir
ou ne vouloir pas, de s'opposer même à sa volonté, lorsqu'il ordonne le bien; cependant ce droit d'opposition,
tout insensé qu'il est, est sacré" (AT, II, 381). Whereas
Voltaire was distrustful of the lower classes and, even in a
democratic government, would have limited participation
to property-holders alone (XVIII, 425), Diderot scorned the
aristocracy and believed that most men who distinguish
themselves in the arts and sciences are of lowly extraction
but are prevented from developing themselves because of
social privileges.[15] Finally, whereas Voltaire sought chiefly

15. Sée, *L'Evolution de la pensée politique,* p. 190. D'Holbach,
despite his conservatism as compared with the revolutionaries of the
end of the century, shares Diderot's democratic views. In his *Politique
naturelle* he decries the privileges of the nobility and proposes the
abolishment of distinctions between "les nobles et les roturiers."
Speaking of his "politique," Daniel Mornet states that the only justi-
fication for authority recognized by the baron is a pact between the

practical liberal reforms within the existing monarchy, Diderot espoused the concept of popular sovereignty and would have preferred to do away with the monarchy completely.[16]

The root of the dichotomy within the Philosophe movement, then, at least so far as Voltaire was concerned,[17] was not in their metaphysical differences but in the practical solutions each side envisaged for the political reform of the

---

nation and the sovereign: "Si le souverain, au lieu de protéger la liberté et de gouverner selon le droit et la raison, prétend exercer un pouvoir despotique et se laisse corrompre par 'les préjugés religieux et politiques' d'Holbach va jusqu'à reconnaître le droit à la révolution ... à tel point que le prudent Naigeon se croit obligé d'atténuer et de rappeler, dans une note, que lorsque les peuples seront éclairés ils auront à leur disposition des moyens 'plus doux' et plus efficaces que les révolutions." *Les Origines intellectuelles de la révolution française* (Paris, 1938), p. 103.

16. An indication of Diderot's hatred of royal power may be had from his poem *Les Eleuthéromanes* (1772), in which he states that if man "osait de son cœur n'écouter que la voix," he would proclaim his freedom, adding: "Et ses mains ourdiraient les entrailles du prêtre, / Au défaut d'un cordon pour étrangler les rois" (AT., IX, 15–16). It is true that in the *Encyclopédie* (see the article "Autorité" [AT., XIII, 392–400], for example), which was composed at an earlier date and with the censors in mind, Diderot's ideal of an enlightened monarch seems to be in harmony with that of Voltaire, and this helps to explain the patriarch's surprise and distress when, as will be seen, he notes the antimonarchic trend which the Holbachic publications take after 1770. But even here the doctrine of the social contract is suggested. According to Mornet, Diderot does not develop a clear political viewpoint until 1767 (*Les Origines*, p. 92). It would be interesting to know whether d'Holbach's strong political views had any influence on this development.

17. Grimm, in speaking of Diderot's objections to Voltaire's "profession de foi de théisme," declares: "C'était l'éternel sujet de leurs querelles." *Mémoires politiques et anecdotiques, inédites, de la cour de France, pendant les règnes de Louis XV et Louis XVI* (Paris, 1830), II, 279. I shall return to this phase of their differences.

nation. In *L'Evolution de la pensée politique* (pp. 384–85), Sée defines this clash of political doctrines as that between liberalism and democracy: the one seeking to avoid despotism in government, the other stressing popular sovereignty and the people's right to change its government. The first manifestation of the dispute, after the Palissot affair in 1760, was on the occasion of the publication by the d'Holbach "manufacture" of Boulanger's *Recherches sur l'origine du despotisme oriental* in January, 1762. Here a new note is struck: not only is the church attacked but the thesis is put forth that religion was born through the complicity of priests and tyrants in order to exploit the credulity of men. The priests make the people think that tyranny is divinely ordained, and the tyrant in return exterminates the enemies of the priests. Upon reading this, Voltaire expresses his disapproval to Damilaville:

Il semble que l'auteur ait tâché de réunir les princes et les prêtres contre lui; il faut tâcher de faire voir au contraire que les prêtres ont toujours été les ennemis des rois. Les prêtres, il est vrai, sont odieux dans ce livre, mais les rois le sont aussi. . . . Rien n'est plus dangereux ni plus maladroit. Je souhaite que le livre ne fasse pas l'effet que je crains; les frères doivent toujours respecter la morale et le trône. La morale est trop blessée dans le livre d'Helvétius, et le trône est trop peu respecté dans ce livre qui lui est dédié. [XLII, 24–25][18]

What particularly disturbed Voltaire was his conviction

18. Voltaire had only recently underlined this attitude by suppressing Meslier's radical political views in the *Extrait des Sentiments de J. Meslier* (1762). Although Boulanger calls a monarchy ruled by law "le chef-d'œuvre de la raison humaine" (*Despotisme oriental*, 1761 ed., p. 421), it is obvious from his condemnation of governments combining church and state that France was far from his ideal, as is underlined by his expression of the hope that some day perfect monarchies will be developed "auxquelles il ne manquera rien de ce qui est de l'essence de ce gouvernement" (p. 425).

that this was not an isolated work but that it announced a new policy toward the throne and that this policy had been forged by Diderot. Franco Venturi says of the "épître dédicatoire" of the *Despotisme oriental*: "Si trattava d'un documento d'energia rara anche in anni posteriori e piú vicina alla fine del secolo. Vi si riflettavo alcune idee tipiche di Boulanger, ma sopratutto la passione di Diderot e di altri del gruppo di d'Holbach. Si trattava d'un vero e proprio manifesto con cui si dava inizio ad una serie di pubblicazioni filosofiche."[19] On his copy, which is now in the Leningrad library, Voltaire completes the heading of the preface, "Lettre de l'auteur à M.——" by inserting: "Helvétius, par M. Diderot"; and at the conclusion of the letter he adds, after "Votre très humble et très obéissant serviteur," "Diderot."[20]

Voltaire's fears for the consequences of this attack on the throne proved justified. Diderot himself admits that although copies are still in circulation, the police are doing their best to stifle the *Despotisme oriental* (AT., XVIII, 62). The inflammatory preface was chiefly to blame for this pursuit and the Diderot-d'Holbach group thought it wisest to have it omitted from future editions. Through Damilaville,

19. "Postille inedite de Voltaire ad alcune opere di Nicolas-Antoine Boulanger e del baron d'Holbach," *Studi Francesi*, V (Maggio–Agosto, 1958), 233.

20. Ibid. Venturi expresses the opinion that the preface is in fact by Diderot. Particularly dangerous was the attack against those in power. Referring to religion as an imposture in the process of dying out, the author of the preface points to those titled political figures who are more enlightened but who nevertheless "crient avec les autres" in order to conserve their political power, adding: "Ce sont, à la vérité, ces gens-là, ce apostats volontaires de la vérité et de la raison, qui seules peuvent être à craindre, si ce n'est pour l'avenir, au moins pour le présent: eux par qui se sont toujours laissés inspirer et conduire les gouvernements faibles" (*Despotisme oriental*, 1761 ed., p. x).

Voltaire was requested to ask his publisher, Cramer, who had printed the *Despotisme,* to suppress the "épître dédicatoire." Voltaire obliged gladly and notified Damilaville that the preface would be omitted from future editions of the book, adding: "Helvétius est véhémentement soupçonné d'avoir fait cet ouvrage. Est-il à Paris, frère Helvétius?" (XLII, 38). The interest in Helvétius was not mere courtesy, as we have seen. The *Despotisme oriental* had threatened to split the Philosophes into opposing camps. Damilaville's request mentioned above must have pleased the patriarch, not only because it proved the wisdom of his criticisms, but because the Diderot faction had turned to him for help in extricating themselves from the dangerous consequences of their bold declaration. This seemed an opportune time to press his advantage and make a strong effort to unite the Philosophes by obtaining assistance with his own plan from Helvétius, who appeared to have some importance in the new publishing venture.[21] Diderot had just pleaded for a united front in the preface of the *Despotisme.* What was more significant, he had expressed a willingness to follow Helvétius' lead in this new "plan de Philosophie politique pour régler les progrès de la Philosophie même" (1761 ed., p. xxiv). Noting that this plan needed "un Philosophe comme vous pour Directeur," he had exclaimed: "Que je travaillerais avec plaisir sous votre puissant génie!" (pp. xxv–xxvi).

Helvétius having failed to respond to his reiterated appeals (see Chapter III), Voltaire sent what Grimm was to label an *Epître aux Fidèles, par le grand apôtre des Délices*

21. Venturi quotes an unpublished manuscript letter from d'Héméry to the director of publications, Malesherbes, saying that the original manuscript of the *Despotisme* has been found in Helvétius' library, "raison pour laquelle M. Helvétius a craint dans ce moment-ci qu'on ne l'en soupçonnât l'auteur, ce qui n'est sûrement pas" ("Postille inedite," p. 232).

(XLII, 513), to both Diderot and the author of *De l'esprit,* calling for a united effort in fighting "le mensonge et la superstition" and with the admonition to avoid metaphysics. In what is apparently a reference to their publication of the *Despotisme oriental* and to its consequences, he reminds his correspondents that those "victims of truth" who allowed books to be published only to have them condemned have a direct interest in accepting his propositions. The letter terminates with a stirring call to unity: "Il paraît donc absolument nécessaire que les sages se défendent, et ils ne peuvent se justifier qu'en éclairant les hommes. Ils peuvent former un corps respectable, au lieu d'être des membres désunis que les fanatiques et les sots hachent en pièces. Il est honteux que la philosophie ne puisse faire chez nous ce qu'elle faisait chez les anciens; elle rassemblait les hommes, et la superstition a seule chez nous ce privilège" (XLII, 513–14). Voltaire's appeal went unanswered, and four months later, on 4 October 1763, he returned to the subject, telling Damilaville: "Je vous avoue, mon cher frère, que je sacrifie tout petit ressentiment, tout intérêt particulier, à ce grand intérêt de la vérité. Il faut assommer une hydre qui a lancé son venin sur tant d'hommes respectables par leurs mœurs et par leur science. Vos amis, et surtout votre principal ami, doivent regarder cette entreprise comme leur premier devoir" (XLIII, 3).

Diderot, despite his silence before these appeals, had become more favorable to Voltaire at this time and had apparently gotten over the resentment that he had felt at the time of the Palissot affair. One factor which brought him closer to the "apôtre des Délices" was the latter's efforts in behalf of the Calas family. In addition to the well known "C'est un sublime ouvrage que *Mahomet*; j'aimerais mieux avoir réhabilité la mémoire de Calas," from his *Neveu de Rameau,* Diderot's correspondence praises Voltaire warmly for this disinterested action (Roth, IV, 97, 142, 247).[22] Voltaire's frequent expressions of esteem and admiration for "Platon" written to Damilaville probably had some effect also, and finally, his aid in the matter of the *Despotisme oriental,* together with his so ardent desire for unity among like-minded men could not help influencing Diderot's attitude. Certainly his reaction to Voltaire's *Traité sur la tolérance* in 1764 suggests that there is now a *rapprochement* between the two groups. He writes to Damilaville asking for twenty-five copies of the *Traité sur la tolérance,* "pour moi et les miens," explaining: "Ils sont tous pour les bienveillants de l'homme et de la cause. Leur devise est aussi: Proscrivez l'Infâme" (Roth, IV, 287).

Within a week, Palissot again threatened to drive a wedge between the two wings of the party by severely attacking Diderot in *La Dunciade.* We have already seen in Chapter III Voltaire's frantic efforts to reassure Damilaville, his awkward attempts to defend his friend Choiseul for protecting both *Les Philosophes* and *La Dunciade,* and finally his desperate and futile attempt once more to have Diderot elected to the Académie française.[23] While neither Damilaville nor Diderot had responded to the admonition not to "braver les puissances de ce monde" (XLIII, 170), d'Alembert, who was still closely linked with their group,[24] had

22. In a letter to Sophie Volland dated 8 August 1762, for example, he mentions the Calas case and exclaims: "C'est de Voltaire qui écrit pour cette malheureuse famille. Oh! mon amie, le bel emploi du génie! Il faut que cet homme ait de l'âme, de la sensibilité, que l'injustice le révolte, et qu'il sente l'attrait de la vertu. . . . Quand il y aurait un Christ, je vous assure que de Voltaire serait sauvé" (Roth, IV, 97).

23. In April, 1764, Diderot speaks of "l'Académie française, dont je ne suis, ni ne serai jamais." In a footnote, Georges Roth comments: "Est-ce là une prophétie ou une décision?—L'événement a confirmé l'une et l'autre, en dépit des efforts de Voltaire" (ibid., p. 293).

24. Roth (ibid., p. 297) records the meeting of the British actor

expressed their disapproval of Voltaire's defense of "les puissances" as well as their disdain for those "qui habitent ces hauts lieux" (XLIII, 179, 185). Yet, perhaps because it was simply an echo of the problems already laid aside after the dispute over *Les Philosophes* in 1760, the second attack, *La Dunciade,* caused less dissension in the Philosophe camp. Indeed, there seems to have been some agreement, resulting from Damilaville's visit to Ferney, to publish polemic brochures under the name of the deceased Boulanger (XLIV, 88). This does not mean, however, that the Diderot group capitulated to the more conservative views of the patriarch: on the contrary, just as Voltaire envisaged the solution of their quarrel in terms of the prodigal son (assuming that the other faction had learned its lesson from the consequences of the *Despotisme oriental,* and was returning to the fold of Ferney), so too Diderot hoped to solve the problem by winning Voltaire over to his own position through their mutual friend Damilaville. During the latter's visit to Ferney, Diderot wrote him a letter reminding him of the atheistic arguments from "ce catéchisme nôtre que vous savez sur le bout du doigt," which he was to recite to his host. Beginning with expressions of admiration for "l'homme incroyable," Diderot then paints the horrors that the "abominable name" of God has visited upon the world, and he concludes: "Dites-lui: . . . pourquoi donc ne prenez-vous pas pour une fausseté, une supposition que vous ne pouvez appliquer à aucune question métaphysique, physique, politique et morale, sans l'obscurcir?"[25]

Three weeks later (6 October 1765), Diderot, in a letter

Garrick with Diderot, d'Alembert, Marmontel, Grimm, Saint-Lambert, and Morellet at the salon of Helvétius. Two years later we find d'Alembert co-operating closely with d'Holbach in connection with the Rousseau-Hume quarrel. See my "Rousseau and d'Alembert."

25. Diderot. *Correspondance inédite,* ed. Babelon (Paris, 1931), I, 278–79.

to Sophie Volland, reveals that his preoccupation is not only with the metaphysical aspects of the question, as is frequently suggested, but with its more concrete application in political and moral terms. In the realm of morality, he hits directly at Voltaire's concept of God as a deterrent to crime: "Un peuple qui croit que c'est la croyance d'un Dieu et non pas les bonnes lois qui font les honnêtes gens ne me paraît guère avancé. . . . La croyance d'un Dieu fait et doit faire presque autant de fanatiques que de croyants. . . . Tôt ou tard, il vient un moment où la notion qui a empêché de voler un écu fait égorger cent mille hommes. Belle compensation!" (AT., XIX, 185–86). The problem of whether morality should stem from religious principles or simply from legislation was to be the most insurmountable obstacle to an agreement between the two factions, and baron d'Holbach was soon to elaborate Diderot's idea in his *Système de la nature*. Another important clue to the future discord in the Philosophe camp can be found in the same letter to Sophie Volland. Whereas Voltaire had held up the English monarchy in an idealized form as a model for France to imitate, d'Holbach had just returned from a trip to England and the picture he painted was quite different from that of the *Lettres philosophiques*. Diderot tells his friend the baron's findings and, after describing the poverty of the people as a result of the favored position of the nobility, the clergy, and exorbitantly opulent merchants, he turns to the political system: "Le monarque paraît avoir les mains libres pour le bien et liées pour le mal; mais il est autant et plus maître de tout qu'aucun autre souverain. Ailleurs la cour commande et se fait obéir. Là, elle corrompt et fait ce qui lui plaît, et la corruption des sujets est peut-être pire à la longue que la tyrannie" (AT., XIX, 182).

Damilaville's visit failed to change Voltaire's basic stand. Two months later he writes Mme du Deffand saying that although he is estranged from several modern philosophers "who dare deny a supreme intelligence," their horror of fanaticism attaches them to him, and he concludes: "Voilà ce qui m'a lié avec des personnes de mérite, qui peut-être ont trop d'inflexibilité dans l'esprit, qui se plient peu aux usages du monde, qui aiment mieux instruire que plaire, qui veulent se faire écouter, et qui dédaignent d'écouter; mais ils rachètent ces défauts par de grandes connaissances et par de grandes vertus" (XLIV, 199).[26] Yet the exchange of arguments had stimulated Voltaire to a renewed interest in the question of the existence of God, and three weeks later (19 February 1766), we find him "plongé dans la métaphysique la plus triste et la plus épineuse." He tells Mme du Deffand that he has begun a search for "ce qui est" (XLIV, 223). The result, *Le Philosophe ignorant*, is a blow-by-blow description of this quest. After rejecting the various philosophies, including that of Spinoza, which attempt to solve the enigma of existence, the patriarch concludes with two truths his reason has shown him. The first is the existence of God: "Rien n'ébranle en moi cet axiome: 'Tout ouvrage démontre un ouvrier'" (XXVI, 59). Characteristically, Voltaire seeks a practical application of this truth, which would be useless if it did not prescribe a rule of conduct in life (XXVI, 78). The second truth therefore has to do with notions of right and wrong and their application to human behavior: "La morale me paraît tellement universelle, tellement calculée par l'Etre universel qui nous a formés, tellement destinée à servir de contrepoids à nos passions funestes, et à soulager les peines inévitables de cette courte vie, que, depuis Zoroastre jusqu'au lord Shaftsbury,

26. A footnote by Beuchot says that "Voltaire veut parler de d'Alembert," but in addition to the fact that d'Alembert was not one of those who denied a supreme intelligence (see D'Al., V, 296, 303), it is more probable that Voltaire was referring to the Diderot-d'Holbach group whose atheism he was preparing to refute.

je vois tous les philosophes enseigner la même morale, quoiqu'ils aient tous des idées différentes sur les principes des choses" (XXVI, 86).

His position having been once more restated, Voltaire set about trying to reconcile the two factions. The La Barre execution gave added impetus to this endeavor and, as we have seen in Chapter IV, he sought to found a Philosophe colony at Clèves, even inviting baron d'Holbach (XLIV, 375), whose rôle in the Diderot faction he may have learned about during Damilaville's visit to Ferney. Diderot's refusal to accept the plan left Voltaire somewhat embittered, and he was once again obliged to rely more heavily on d'Alembert in his campaign against "l'Infâme." In reply to his *Philosophe ignorant,* and as if to underline the differences which stood in the way of co-operative action, the d'Holbach "manufacture" launched its own campaign of clandestine publications beginning with the *Christianisme dévoilé* in the same year (1766).[27]

27. There had been a first edition of *Le Christianisme dévoilé,* printed in Nancy in 1761, but it does not seem to have been widely circulated. There is no mention of the work by Voltaire until the appearance of the 1766 edition. In December, 1766, he tells Mme de Saint-Julien that she is welcome to see his marginal notes to his copy of the work as proof of his objection to its atheism (XLIV, 534–35; the marginal comments are given in XXXI, 129). Venturi has published Voltaire's marginal comments in his copy of the London 1767 edition located at the Leningrad library. *Studi Francesi,* V (1958), 231–37. Babelon states of *Le Christianisme dévoilé* "La Harpe assure que cet ouvrage aurait été composé en grande partie d'après la conversation de Diderot. Ce dernier en fut en tout cas l'éditeur." Diderot, *Corres. inéd.,* I, 226. Topazio suggests, on the other hand, not only that Diderot had nothing to do with the work, but that he was even unaware of d'Holbach's authorship. "Diderot's Supposed Contribution to d'Holbach's Works," *PMLA,* LXIX (March, 1954), 174–76, 187. The article is a healthy antidote to the traditional tendency to make Diderot d'Holbach's ghostwriter for the better passages in his works. However, in seeking to separate Diderot entirely from the

The *Christianisme dévoilé* was the opening shot in the
battle to come. Here was not simply an attack on Christianity and its priests but on religion in general, and what
was more significant, on the notion that religious principles
are useful for the good conduct of society. The preface,
which is an appeal to Voltaire to abandon his deism for the
atheists' position, developed the view shared, as we have

clandestine publication venture of d'Holbach and Naigeon the better
to vindicate d'Holbach's authorship, Topazio may have weakened his
case by attempting to explain away what evidence does exist to warrant such a link. To this end he delves into conjectures which can be
disputed. Thus Diderot's letter to Falconet in 1767 asking who, in his
opinion, wrote the work, and Grimm's expressions of ignorance in his
Correspondance littéraire as to who might be responsible for "cette
manufacture" are taken at face value and represented as evidence for
the view that Diderot and Grimm were unaware of the whole venture
("Diderot's Supposed Contribution," p. 175). Yet there is an equally
valid and plausible interpretation of the statements. Since an author
publishing such dangerous works would be, in the words of Grimm,
"fou à lier de jouer son repos et son bonheur" (Grimm, *Correspondance littéraire, philosophique et critique,* ed. Tourneux [Paris, 1877–
1882] VII, 426), a close friend of such an author would be the last one
to jeopardize his friend's peace and happiness by betraying his ano-
nymity, all the more so if he himself were directly involved. The wisest
course would be to pretend complete ignorance of the impious author.
This is not to say that Diderot *did* take part in the publication venture
—although the inclusion of his *Pensées sur la religion* in Naigeon's
two-volume *Recueil philosophique* (1770) is further evidence in favor
of such a view—but it simply indicates that the contrary view has yet
to be proved conclusively, and sufficient evidence exists to warrant
accepting the tentative thesis that Diderot was cognizant of and perhaps active in the d'Holbach "manufacture." Certainly Grimm was
sufficiently aware of the source of the *Christianisme dévoilé* to mock
Voltaire's reply, the *Homélie* on atheism. Pomeau states that the rebuttal "lui attire derechef les ricanements dédaigneux de la *Correspondance littéraire.* Le journaliste veut bien nous faire connaître la
condamnation fulminée par l'Eglise métropolitaine et primatiale des
athées de Paris'; il fut déclaré que 'le patriarche, avec son rémunérateur et punisseur, n'était qu'un capucin. . . .' " *La Religion,* p. 389.

seen, with Diderot, that religion was not necessary for con-
trolling the masses. It was not true that it was an essential
curb for crude or simple minds: "C'est la loi qui contient
les gens du peuple et quand un insensé leur dirait de voler
ou d'assassiner, le gibet les avertirait de n'en rien faire."[28]
D'Holbach then refutes Voltaire's objections to atheism and
announces his intention to attack religion as a citizen because it is detrimental to the welfare of the state, an enemy
of human progress, and opposed to true morality which
cannot be separated from political considerations (p. xxvii).
On this level, Voltaire had no alternative but to join the
atheists or attack them, and the conclusion of d'Holbach's
preface presents him with just such an ultimatum: "Si tibi
vera videtur, / Dede manus, et si falsa est, accingere contra"
(p. xxviii).[29]

Voltaire's opinion of the *Christianisme dévoilé* is well
summed up in a letter dated 15 December 1766, in which
he denies having written the work, saying: ". . . je serais
très fâché de l'avoir fait, non seulement comme académicien, mais comme philosophe, et encore plus comme
citoyen." The book is entirely opposed to his principles, he
explains, because it leads to atheism, which is clearly unreasonable. It would be as ridiculous to say that a well-
ordered universe does not prove a "supreme artisan" as to
say that a watch does not prove a watchmaker. The patriarch concludes: "Je ne réprouve pas moins ce livre comme
citoyen; l'auteur paraît trop ennemi des puissances. Des

28. Original edition, p. v. The title page is dated "Londres
MDCCLVI" and the preface antedated "mai 1758," but W. H. Wickwar indicates that it actually was printed in Nancy in 1761. *Baron
d'Holbach: a Prelude to the French Revolution* (London, 1935), p.
239.

29. On his copy now at the Leningrad library, Voltaire com-
mented: "Plate préface—elle rend nécessaire ce que l'auteur veut
combattre." Venturi, "Postille inedite," p. 236.

hommes qui penseraient comme lui ne formeraient qu'une anarchie" (XLIV, 534–35). The challenge of d'Holbach's preface to join the fight or become an adversary is answered in the *Homélies prononcées à Londres* early the following year. The "Première homélie: sur l'athéisme" stresses the social utility of a belief in God by countering d'Holbach's view that laws alone are sufficient to curb crime. An atheist, says Voltaire, will have no remorse for his crime and will remain a criminal, whereas a believer will reform: "Le premier est un monstre pour toute sa vie, le second n'aura été barbare qu'un moment. Pourquoi? C'est que l'un a un frein, l'autre n'a rien qui l'arrête." He concludes: "L'idée d'un Dieu vengeur est donc nécessaire" (XXVI, 323).

The remaining "Homélies" deal with Biblical criticism and the distinctions between theism and fanaticism, and terminate with a plea to "les fidèles" to avoid too violent an attack on their mutual enemies. In a statement, reminiscent of d'Alembert's suggestion years earlier that a light must be introduced into a cave slowly or the inhabitants will reject it as harmful, the author exhorts the faithful: "Rejetons donc toute superstition afin de devenir plus humains; mais en parlant contre le fanatisme, n'irritons point les fanatiques: ce sont des malades en délire qui veulent battre leurs médecins. Adoucissons leurs maux, ne les aigrissons jamais, et faisons couler goutte à goutte dans leur âme ce baume divin de la tolérance, qu'ils rejetteraient avec horreur si on le leur présentait à pleine coupe" (XXVI, 354).

Three months later d'Alembert writes Voltaire announcing d'Holbach's *Théologie portative* (XLV, 353), and on 22 September 1767 he exclaims: "Il nous pleut ici de Hollande des ouvrages sans nombre contre l'infâme," and he lists the anonymously published *L'Esprit du clergé, Les Prêtres démasqués,* the *Théologie portative,* and *Le Militaire philosophe* (XLV, 380). Inasmuch as the Holbachic

publications at this time were less concerned with building
the atheistic state than with destroying the religious basis
of the existing one,[30] their objectives seemed to coincide
with those of Voltaire. He therefore answered d'Alembert's
letters joyously. The priests are being laughed at in the
streets; everyone is reading those books, he replies. Pretending to be a believer, he writes facetiously to his lieutenant
in a subsequent letter lamenting the attacks against Christianity and attributing them to "des jeunes gens et des
moines défroqués." As for d'Holbach's anonymous *L'Imposture sacerdotale*, he tells d'Alembert: ". . . vous y verrez
le style de Démosthène" (XLV, 524–26).

Yet, it was an uneasy joy which the new works brought
him. The differences between their objectives and his were
becoming only too apparent, and Voltaire felt himself drawn
more and more into open conflict with the atheistic group
in Paris. His *Profession de foi des Théistes* and his "Homélie" on atheism had earned him "les ricanements dédaigneux de la *Correspondance littéraire*."[31] The epithet of
"capucin" by the atheists of Paris was countered by the
Colimaçons du R. P. l'Escarbotier, followed by *Les Singu-
larités de la nature*, and *L'A, B, C*. In spite of this exchange,
Voltaire had not given up hope of mending the widening
rift between the two groups, and he began seeking a compromise.[32] His *A, B, C*, for example, despite its forceful
reiteration of his basic position: "Oui, têtebleue, je crois

30. Topazio calls this period "the destructive phase of the baron's
attacks upon religion," and explains that d'Holbach "launched his
attack upon religion as the practical means of laying the groundwork
for the type of morality he considered capable of realizing the kind
of world he envisioned." *D'Holbach's Moral Philosophy*, pp. 21, 23.

31. Pomeau, *La Religion*, p. 389.

32. Pomeau states (ibid., p. 408): "Aussi Voltaire envisageait-il
d'accorder sa pensée à celle de Diderot." For a detailed and accurate
view of Voltaire's strong desire for accord with Diderot and the latter's
cooler attitude, see Torrey's "Voltaire's Reaction."

en Dieu" (XXVII, 399), reveals nevertheless a preoccupation with winning his opponents through their own authorities. Such statements as: "Encore une fois, Spinosa lui-même admet cette intelligence," occur periodically. The idea that the world co-existed with God from all eternity and is "une émanation éternelle de lui-même" is put forth (XXVII, 396), showing to what extent he had abandoned his earlier concept of the Newtonian world machine created *ex nihilo*. D'Alembert, who was as impatient with metaphysical speculation as his master had been, notices Voltaire's hedging and exclaims: ". . . on nous a envoyé il y a peu de jours *l'a, b, c;* c'est un tissu de dialogues sur tout ce qui a été, est, et sera. Dans le dernier dialogue l'auteur soupçonne qu'il pourrait bien y avoir un Dieu, et qu'en même temps le monde est éternel; il parle de tout cela en homme qui ne sait pas trop bien ce qui en est. Je crois qu'il dirait volontiers comme ce capitaine suisse à un déserteur qu'on allait pendre, et qui lui demandait s'il y avait un autre monde: 'par la mort-dieu, je donnerais bien cent écus pour le savoir' " (D'Al., V, 281).

Diderot once wrote: ". . . je ne suis aucunement tyran des opinions, je dis mes raisons et j'attends; j'ai remarqué plusieurs fois au bout d'un certain temps que mon adversaire et moi nous avions tous les deux changé d'avis" (AT., XIX, 477). Had this been the case in his quarrel with Voltaire, a middle ground might well have been reached; but, although the patriarch proved willing to accept much of Diderot's stand, the latter remained adamant. Basically, Voltaire's compromise solution was their mutual acceptance of a Spinozistic concept of the universe. His *Tout en Dieu* (1769), despite its subtitle, "Commentaire sur Malebranche," is actually an exposition of Spinoza's philosophy. When he sends a copy to d'Alembert on 15 August 1769 he writes: "Personne n'imagine que saint Paul et Nicolas Malebranche approchassent du spinosisme; c'est à vous d'en

juger. Il faut que Benoît Spinoza ait été un esprit bien con-
ciliant, car je vois que tout le monde retombe malgré soi
dans les idées de ce mauvais Juif" (XLVI, 414). To which
d'Alembert replied: "Il y a bien longtemps que je suis persuadé que Jean Scot, Malebranche, et tous ces rêveurs, ou
ne savaient pas ce qu'ils étaient, ou étaient réellement
spinosistes; et qu'à l'égard de Spinosa, ou toute sa métaphysique ne signifie rien, ou elle signifie que la matière est
la seule chose existante, et que c'est dans elle qu'il faut
chercher ou supposer la raison de tout" (XLVI, 423–24).
Was this a warning to Voltaire that his new Spinozistic outlook would eventually lead him to the materialistic position
of his opponents? He himself was aware of this danger when,
in his dialogue between *Sophronime et Adélos* (1766), he
suggested that such a concept of God "ne sera plus aux yeux
de bien des philosophes qu'une force secrète répandue dans
la nature; nous retomberons peut-être dans le matérialisme
de Straton en voulant l'éviter" (XXV, 466).

We have already seen that Voltaire refused to follow his
own tendencies to the point of denying the existence of God
altogether. D'Alembert during this same period was under-
going a similar "crise de conscience." Prior to the metaphysical arguments brought on by the publication of the
Christianisme dévoilé, d'Alembert had rejected the materialists' theory of the chance formation of the universe
from matter in motion and had reflected an attitude similar
to that of Voltaire; i.e., a universe in which intelligence and
design appear cannot be the work of chance.[33] In his reply
to Voltaire concerning *Tout en Dieu*, the geometer had referred his friend to the passage in his *Mélanges de philosophie* just mentioned and had ended his remarks with his
usual conclusion in such questions: since no clear idea can
be had on matter or anything else, only skepticism is reasonable (XLVI, 424).

That same year, 1769, Diderot wrote his *Entretien entre*

33. D'Alembert, *Œuvres inéd.*, ed. Henry, pp. 18–19.

Diderot et d'Alembert, with its sequel, the *Rêve de d'Alembert.* Had d'Alembert attempted to defend his skeptical deism before Diderot in baron d'Holbach's salon? And was this Diderot's rebuttal? The authentic ring of the arguments which Diderot places in d'Alembert's mouth in his *Entretien* as well as the author's attempt to prevent the geometer's retreat behind his usual skepticism by denying the possibility of such a position lend credence to such an assumption.[34] It suffices to say here that two years later, commenting to Frederick on the monarch's refutation of d'Holbach's *Système de la nature,* d'Alembert, when pressed further,[35] reflects a position close to that expounded in Diderot's *Rêve.* Admitting the eternity of matter, he goes to the problem of intelligence: "Cette intelligence dans l'homme et dans les animaux, est-elle distinguée de la matière, ou n'en est-elle qu'une propriété dépendante de l'organisation? L'expérience paraît prouver, et même démontrer le dernier, puisque l'intelligence croît et s'éteint, à mesure que l'organisation se perfectionne et s'affaiblit." He

34. We know that d'Alembert read the manuscript of the *Entretien* and *Rêve* because, at the request of Mlle de Lespinasse, who was offended by it, he insisted that Diderot destroy the work (AT., II, 104). The relations between Diderot and d'Alembert will be explored more fully in a subsequent study.

35. In a previous letter d'Alembert had given Frederick his stock reply when asked for an opinion. In metaphysics, "la devise de Montaigne, 'que sais-je?' me paraît la réponse qu'on doit faire à presque toutes les questions de ce genre." And, inasmuch as the monarch, in his rebuttal of d'Holbach's *Système,* had defended Voltaire's theism, the geometer began with his prudent admission that in the universe and in the structure of animals and plants there were "des combinaisons de parties qui semblent déceler une intelligence, comme une montre prouve l'existence d'un horloger; cela paraît incontestable: mais . . ." (D'Al., V, 296). Unlike that of Zadig, however, d'Alembert's "mais" was followed by so many arguments favoring materialism that Frederick felt obliged to answer them. The geometer then wrote a more frank exposition of his opinion, prefacing it with the suggestion that in reality both were in agreement.

then concludes: "Nous sommes donc réduits, avec la meilleure volonté du monde, à ne reconnaître et n'admettre tout au plus dans l'univers qu'un Dieu matériel, borné et dépendant;[36] je ne sais pas si c'est là son compte, mais ce n'est sûrement pas celui des partisans zélés de l'existence de Dieu; ils nous aimeraient autant athées que spinosistes, comme nous le sommes. Pour les adoucir, faisons-nous sceptiques, et répétons avec Montaigne, 'que sais-je?' " (D'Al., V, 303–4). Frederick refused to accept d'Alembert's argument for a material God but insisted that God was "the intelligence attached to the eternal organization of the worlds in existence," to which the Academician replied that God, according to such a definition, is that part of matter which is intelligent, and he concludes: ". . . on est très libre de donner le nom de Dieu à la matière en tant que doué de cet attribut" (D'Al., V, 308).

Apparently, d'Alembert attempted to use similar arguments with Voltaire when he visited him at Ferney. Du Pan, writing of Voltaire in his *Mémoires,* tells of witnessing such a discussion at the time, as follows: "Je l'ai vu un soir à souper, donner une énergique leçon à d'Alembert et à Condorcet, en renvoyant tous ses domestiques de l'appartement, au milieu du repas, et en disant ensuite aux deux académiciens: 'Maintenant, Messieurs, continuez vos propos contre Dieu; mais comme je ne veux pas être égorgé et volé cette nuit par mes domestiques, il est bon qu'ils ne vous écoutent pas."[37] If the anecdote is true, we can imagine d'Alembert, with his admiration of consistency in a philo-

36. Cf. Diderot's *Rêve*: "Mlle de L'Espinasse: 'Comment cette espèce de Dieu-là. . . .' Bordeu: 'La seule qui se conçoive. . . .' Mlle de L.: 'Pourrait avoir été, ou venir et passer?' Bordeu: 'Sans doute; mais puisqu'il serait matière dans l'univers, portion de l'univers, sujet à vicissitudes, il vieillirait, il mourrait' " (AT., II, 142–43).

37. *Mémoires et correspondance de Mallet du Pan* (Paris, 1851), I, 50–51.

sophy,[38] pointing out the inconsistencies in Voltaire's writings; but, knowing his care to avoid offending his friend, one may suppose that his arguments probably were presented with the same circumspection which he had used with Frederick.[39]

38. When discussing Voltaire's *Tout en Dieu* with his "cher maître," d'Alembert, after affirming that either Spinoza's metaphysics signifies nothing or it means that matter is the only thing in existence, had explained: "Je sais que ce sentiment est abominable, mais du moins il s'entend, et c'est quelque chose en philosophie que de savoir au moins ce qu'on veut dire, quand on ne sait pas ce qu'on doit dire." Concerning Descartes's denial of the existence in animals of a principle distinguished from matter, d'Alembert, despite his rejection of Cartesian philosophy, commends its author for being "le plus conséquent" of philosophers writing on that subject (XLVI, 424). Diderot, too, admired a "philosophie claire, nette et franche," such as that expounded by d'Holbach: "L'auteur du *Système de la nature* n'est pas athée dans une page, déiste dans une autre: sa philosophie est tout d'une pièce. On ne lui dira pas: Tâchez de vous entendre . . ." (AT., II, 398).

39. Even when he disliked certain of Voltaire's works d'Alembert avoided telling him so. When, in 1763, for example, Voltaire sent him his latest works, d'Alembert thanked him for the *Lettre du Quaker,* saying: ". . . c'est apparemment un de vos amis de Philadelphie qui vous a chargé de me faire ce cadeau-là; il ne pouvait choisir une voie plus agréable pour moi de me faire parvenir sa petite remontrance à Jean-Georges. . . . Je vous remercie de plus, mon cher philosophe, de vos excellentes *Additions à l'Histoire générale,* non seulement de celles que vous avez refondues dans l'ouvrage, mais de celles que vous avez données à part en un petit volume, et qui m'ont paru excellentes" (XLIII, 43–44). But to Mlle de Lespinasse, as we have seen, he said the *Additions* were "à faire vomir par la bassesse et la platitude de ses éloges," and turning to the *Lettre* he added: "Il est bien digne après cela d'avoir fait une platte parodie de réquisitoire d'Omer, qu'il était si aisé de tourner en ridicule. . . ." *Œuvres inéd.,* ed. Henry, p. 292. Similarly, despite the depreciating manner in which he speaks of *L'A,B,C,* to Frederick (as quoted previously), d'Alembert writes to Voltaire the very next day: "J'ai lu, il y a quelques jours, une brochure intitulée l'A,B,C; j'ai été charmé surtout de ce qu'on y dit sur la guerre et sur la liberté naturelle" (XLVI, 194).

If Voltaire in fact knew d'Alembert's true metaphysical
position, it may help to explain why he thought his disciple
was the one who could effect a reconciliation with a group
whose views he shared. For, in reality, it was not the "athée
de cabinet" the patriarch was fighting, but those who dis-
seminated their opinions publicly. Such principles would
lead eventually to a "prince athée," and there was the danger (XVIII, 380). Besides, d'Alembert did not hold dog-
matically to atheism and revealed his personal leanings only
to intimate friends, while fostering his master's position as
an official policy; this was all Voltaire asked. But even those
who publicly professed atheism were treated with some indulgence by Voltaire. True, he considered the materialist
position which substituted for a universal intelligence an
incomprehensible nature and impossible calculations to be
a "galimatias qui fait pitié"; but still, those philosophers
had something excellent about them: "Leur horreur pour
le fanatisme et leur amour de la tolérance m'attache à eux.
Ces deux points doivent leur concilier l'amitié de tous les
honnêtes gens" (XLVI, 300). In order to regain their friendship he had changed his own position to the point of saying
of those who only admitted the secret power of nature: "Je
suis de leur avis, pourvu qu'ils reconnaissent que ce pouvoir
secret est celui d'un Etre nécessaire, éternel, puissant, intelligent" (XXX, 475). This d'Alembert had always maintained as a practical, official position, and even when suggesting materialism, he always fell back on his convenient
"Que sais-je?" as a conclusion.

Voltaire's refusal to abandon his belief in a supreme intelligence earned him the scorn not only of Grimm's *Correspondance littéraire* but of the whole d'Holbach coterie
in Paris. Diderot is reported to have called him a "cagot"
(XXXVII, 23). Walpole writes during a trip to Paris in 1765
that the group is openly preaching atheism: "Voltaire himself doesn't satisfy them. One of their lady devotees said of

him, 'Il est bigot, c'est un déiste.' "[40] Joseph Priestley, while
reminiscing about his trip to France in 1774, speaks of the
attitude of the atheists toward Voltaire, who "was considered by them as a weak-minded man, because, though an
unbeliever in revelation, he believed in a God."[41] Paradoxically, the activities of the atheists in Paris were precisely
what Voltaire himself had been urging right along. He had
frequently accused the Philosophes of being lukewarm and
lacking in zeal. Here at last, in baron d'Holbach, was a
zealot who seemed like the incarnation of the patriarch's
desires. Horace Walpole testifies to the baron's missionary
fervor when he calls him and his group "fanatics," explaining: ". . . they preach incessantly, and their avowed doctrine
is atheism." Walpole finally ceased attending the baron's
dinners because "there was no bearing the authors, and
philosophers and 'savants,' of which he had a pigeon-house
full. They soon turned my head with a new system of ante-
diluvian deluges, which they have invented to prove the
eternity of matter. The Baron is persuaded that Pall Mall is
paved with lava or deluge stones."[42]

Diderot is said to have remarked about d'Holbach: ". . .
quelque système que forge mon imagination, je suis sûr que
mon ami d'Holbach me trouve des faits et des autorités
pour le justifier."[43] As the theorist of the group, d'Holbach
brought to their logical conclusions ideas which Voltaire

40. *The Letters of Horace Walpole,* ed. Toynbee, VI, 352.
41. Quoted by Bernard N. Schilling, *Conservative England and
the Case Against Voltaire* (New York, 1950), p. 198. Schilling presents
many more reports from English travelers of the Philosophes' attitude
toward Voltaire.
42. *Letters,* ed. Toynbee, VI, 352, 370.
43. André Cazes, *Grimm et les encyclopédistes* (Paris, 1933), p. 223.
René Hubert says of d'Holbach: ". . . il usait d'une logique vigoureuse
qui lui permettait, les prémisses de la doctrine une fois posées, d'en
tirer toutes les conséquences." *D'Holbach et ses amis* (Paris, 1928),
p. 74.

himself had put forth as early as 1734 in his *Lettres philoso-phiques*. Thus, the Lockean principles affirmed by Voltaire led, as we have seen, to a materialistic explanation of the universe. Yet when Diderot, and later d'Holbach, developed his statements into a coherent system, Voltaire recoiled in horror. When the atheists developed more formally his own utilitarian concept of virtue as obedience to law, he again objected and affirmed his Cartesian-like belief in fixed, eternal principles engraved in the hearts of all men.[44] Although he wished to spare the king in his attacks and considered the church as the real culprit in his campaign, his exposition of the abuses in the monarchy led others to conclude, perhaps with more perspicacity, that the monarchy and the church were so interrelated that both had to be attacked simultaneously. When the atheistic coterie expressed this view, again Voltaire decried it as a dangerous proposal. His reactions are understandable. He was interested not in abstract systems but in meeting concrete problems as they emerged. The principles he had utilized throughout his long polemic career had not necessarily represented his own inner convictions but had been used more or less indiscriminately if they served his purpose in a given dispute. When attacking orthodox dogmas, for example, he had found it expedient to utilize concepts which, when turned against his own religious views, forced him into the awkward position of rejecting some of his own previously stated principles. It is not surprising that the atheistic Philo-

44. Crocker gives a good exposition of the contradiction in Voltaire's view on virtue in "Voltaire's Struggle for Humanism," pp. 156–160. Commenting on Voltaire's statement: "La grande affaire et la seule qu'on doive avoir, c'est de vivre heureux," Crocker remarks: "It is true, however, that when d'Holbach drew (abstractly) from the hedonistic premise a conclusion of moral nihilism, Voltaire revolted and declared virtue to be the highest value, essential to the preservation of society" (p. 160).

sophes saw in Voltaire's stubborn insistence on a belief in God a weakness and an evidence of the "superstition" they were combatting. His Easter communions in 1768 and 1769 were to reinforce the conclusion stated by d'Holbach in the *Système de la nature* a year later, and which he aimed directly at the patriarch: "Il n'y aura jamais qu'un pas du Théisme à la superstition."[45]

The delayed-action fuse lighted by Voltaire in 1734 with his *Lettres philosophiques* was to set off in 1770 what René Pomeau calls, in his *Religion de Voltaire* (p. 389), "la bombe du *Système de la nature*." This was not simply another in the series of Holbachic works. It was, in the words of René Hubert, "un compendium de tous les arguments que la métaphysique des sciences naturelles pouvait invoquer au XVIIIe siècle en faveur des hypothèses matérialistes."[46] The accuracy of this view is reinforced by the striking similarity between the views of d'Holbach and Diderot. We have already alluded to the Holbachic ideas contained in some of

45. *Système de la nature* (Londres, 1770), II, 216. Attributing the various concepts of God to variations in temperament caused by "les humeurs," d'Holbach concludes: "Ainsi le Théisme, ou la prétendu 'religion naturelle,' ne peut avoir des principes sûrs, et ceux qui la professent sont nécessairement sujets à varier dans leurs opinions sur la Divinité et sur la conduite qui en déroule. Leur système, fondé dans l'origine sur un Dieu sage, intelligent, dont la bonté ne peut jamais se démentir, dès que les circonstances viennent à changer, doit bientôt se convertir en fanatisme et en superstition." Ibid., p. 217.

46. *D'Holbach et ses amis*, p. 74. Topazio has argued convincingly, in the works previously cited, against the tradition that Diderot wrote the more readable parts of the *Système*. In view of the long and ardent debates on atheism for which the d'Holbach salon was noted, Hubert's conclusion (pp. 73–74) seems to be the most plausible. D'Holbach's rôle was to "alourdir en système" the scattered arguments and views of such habitués as Diderot, Duclos, Naigeon, Saint-Lambert, *et al.* D'Holbach doubtless wrote the *Système* himself but it reflected and synthesized the ideas which he held in common with the members of his "synagogue."

the Encyclopedist's correspondence. Georges Roth points to a long letter from Diderot in 1756 as "un résumé du chapitre XII de d'Holbach sur la liberté, dans son *Système de la nature*" (Roth, I, 215). Voltaire himself, even though as early as 1768 he knew that it was "un baron d'Holbach qui fait venir toutes les brochures imprimées à Amsterdam chez Marc-Michel Rey" (XLVI, 4), could still be uncertain of the authorship of the *Essai sur les préjugés* in 1770, and even suggests Diderot as its author (XLVII, 104). It was natural for Voltaire, and for many of his contemporaries, to suspect Diderot of being the moving spirit behind the atheistic campaign. Daniel Mornet emphasizes Diderot's rôle in the diffusion of the "bold" doctrines of materialism by explaining that among those who proclaimed it Morelly was obscure and d'Holbach was unknown as a writer: not twenty people suspected he was the author of the *Système de la nature*. On the other hand, the *Pensées philosophiques* with its concluding "Prière matérialiste," and even Morelly's *Code de la nature* had appeared under Diderot's name.[47]

The *Système* aroused a bitter attack against the materialists from the "parti dévot." In an obvious appeal to Voltaire and other deists, the "assemblée du clergé" called upon even those who had heretofore joined in the author's attacks against religion to help refute "ce système audacieux et révoltant."[48] Voltaire, caught between the two warring factions, actually rallied to the call whether he intended to or not. Abbé Galiani, a frequenter of d'Holbach's salon, appears amused at the patriarch's predicament when, in 1772, he receives a copy of *Il faut prendre un parti*. The abbé writes: "C'est bien plaisant qu'on soit parvenu à un point que Voltaire paraisse modéré dans ses opinions, et qu'il se flatte d'être compté parmi les protecteurs de la religion et

47. *Les Origines*, pp. 230–31.
48. Quoted (by Pomeau, *La Religion*, p. 391) from the *Avertissement du clergé*, 1770, p. 17.

qu'il faille, au lieu de le persécuter, le protéger et l'encourager."[49]

Voltaire's early reaction to the *Système* was, however, somewhat uncertain. Upon learning that Frederick of Prussia is composing a refutation (XLVII, 132), Voltaire first tries to sound out Grimm (XLVII, 124) and d'Alembert (XLVII, 139) on their reactions. To the latter he says of the book: ". . . il me paraît qu'il y a des choses excellentes, une raison forte, et de l'éloquence mâle, et que par conséquent il fera un mal affreux à la philosophie" (XLVII, 439). D'Alembert replied that he agreed that it was a "terrible book," adding: ". . . je vous avoue que sur l'existence de Dieu, l'auteur me paraît trop ferme et trop dogmatique, et je ne vois en cette matière que le scepticisme de raisonnable" (XLVII, 451). Before d'Alembert's letter had reached him, Voltaire, perhaps because Frederick was "fâché que les philosophes ne soient pas royalistes," had realized the danger latent in the *Système*: "Je ne trouve pas ces messieurs adroits: ils attaquent à la fois Dieu et le diable, les grands et les prêtres." The opposition of "Dieu" and "les grands" to "le diable" and "les prêtres" betrays the patriarch's basic attitude in the fight against "l'Infâme," and points up an important reason for his conclusion: "Voilà une guerre civile entre les incrédules" (XLVII, 153). D'Alembert shows the same concern for the practical consequences of such a direct attack against both religion and the crown when he replies: "Je vous ai déjà mandé mon sentiment sur le *Système de la nature*; 'non,' en métaphysique, ne me paraît guère plus sage que 'oui'; 'non liquet' est la seule réponse raisonnable à presque tout. D'ailleurs,

49. Abbé F. Galiani, *Correspondance avec Mme d'Epinay, Mme Necker, Mme Geoffrin, etc.*, ed. Perey and Maugras (Paris, 1881), II, 103-4. See Pomeau, *La Religion*, pp. 391-92, for the use of Voltaire's writings against atheists made by such anti-Philosophes as Chaudon and abbés Bonafois and Flexier de Reval.

indépendamment de l'incertitude de la matière, je ne sais si on fait bien d'attaquer directement et ouvertement certains points auxquels il serait peut-être mieux de ne pas toucher" (XLVII, 162).

In his *La Religion* (p. 390), René Pomeau, in reference to d'Alembert's visit to Ferney in September, 1770, queries: "Que fit-il savoir à Voltaire?" and in answer he quotes the patriarch's statement: "Bien des choses que j'ignorais." What were these things? Why, after d'Alembert's visit, did he enter into an unrestrained campaign against the d'Holbach coterie? Perhaps a more thorough review of the geometer's reaction to the *Système* and the tactics of the group for which it spoke might suggest some answers to these unresolved questions.

Several months before the publication of the *Système*, d'Alembert had already begun to voice his disapproval of the harsh attacks emanating from the d'Holbach "boutique." In March, 1770, when discussing Fontenelle's statement that even if he held the truth in his hand he would never open it, d'Alembert had rejected it as an extreme and had put forth his own idea for gradual enlightenment: the hand must not be kept closed but must be opened wisely and with caution, one finger at a time, until it is eventually completely opened and the whole truth has come out. But he had also rejected the opposite extreme: "Les philosophes qui ouvrent la main trop brusquement sont des fous; on leur coupe le poing et voilà tout ce qu'ils gagnent: mais ceux qui la tiennent fermée absolument, ne font pas pour l'humanité ce qu'ils doivent" (D'Al., V, 290-91). The following month, d'Alembert continued to expound his method in a letter to Frederick. Asserting that superstitions should not be attacked violently, the Academician suggests that one must use finesse and patience. Error should be attacked indirectly, by establishing contrary truths on solid principles but without making any direct applications. He then concludes: "Il ne faut pas braquer le canon contre la maison, parce que ceux qui la défendent tireraient des fenêtres une grêle de coups de fusil; il faut petit à petit élever à côté une autre maison plus habitable et plus commode; insensiblement tout le monde viendra habiter celle-ci, et la maison pleine de léopards sera désertée" (D'Al., V, 293).

The appearance of d'Holbach's *Essai sur les préjugés* evoked a refutation from Frederick of Prussia. D'Alembert, in an attempt to disassociate himself and his party from this radical group of Philosophes, agrees with the monarch and informs him that the precautions taken by the government to prevent the sale of such books actually honor the authors more than they are worth and only insure higher sales for the work. As for the brochures and books against what Voltaire calls "XXX," he pursues, he is tired of them and is tempted to say of the title of "philosophe" what Jacques Rosbif says of that of "Monsieur" in the play *Le Français à Londres*: ". . . je ne veux point de ce titre-là, il y a trop de faquins qui le portent." The reason for such an attitude is apparent in the next statement: "On peut dire de tous nos écrivailleurs contre la superstition et le despotisme, ce que le P. de La Rue, jésuite, disait de son confrère Le Tellier: 'il nous mène si grand train qu'il nous versera' " (D'Al., V, 294).

D'Alembert's disapproval of the *Système,* as we have seen, was less for metaphysical reasons than for practical considerations. His strongest statement on the work was made several years after its appearance, when he informed Voltaire that Frederick had cooled toward the Philosophe movement because, "Il ne lui a pas pardonné le *Système de la nature,* dont l'auteur en effet a fait une grande sottise de réunir, contre la philosophie, les princes et les prêtres, en leur persuadant, très mal à propos, selon moi, qu'ils font bourse et

cause communes. Il y a partout des gâte-métiers, et cet
écrivain en est un" (L, 335).[50] Fearing that his frequenting
of d'Holbach's salon might cause the authorities to consider him one of those who were preaching against Church
and Crown, d'Alembert ceased to have any connection with
the group and sought to preserve his own little "église"
from suspicion.[51]

It is quite probable that one of the things d'Alembert
suggested to Voltaire during his stay at Ferney was that, because of the opposed methods that each group had adopted,
reconciliation was impossible and, in any case, would have
been undesirable from the point of view of the cause. A
further suggestion of what d'Alembert might have told
Voltaire during his visit may be found in the latter's numerous statements against the *Système* following this event. Perhaps the most often repeated affirmation is the one he makes
to Mme du Deffand shortly after d'Alembert's departure:

50. Still later, in 1775, d'Alembert returned to the subject when
discussing the coronation of Louis XVI. He remarks that the "impu-
dent" priests who omitted the custom of asking the people whether
they recognized their new king would sever if they could the bond
of love uniting subjects to their monarch, and he adds: "Je sais bien
mauvais gré à l'auteur du *Système de la nature* du prétendu pacte
qu'il imagine que les rois ont fait avec les prêtres pour opprimer les
peuples; si cet écrivain dangereux eût seulement ouvert *L'Histoire
ecclésiastique,* il y aurait vu que de tout temps et en toute occasion
les prêtres ont été les plus grands ennemis des rois" (D'Al., V, 364),
On Voltaire's death in 1778, d'Alembert again shows his resentment
against d'Holbach's work when, after remarking that the clergy were
too stupid to see the advantage they could have had by burying Voltaire in Paris with his profession of faith engraved on his tomb, he
adds: "Ils ont pourtant eu l'esprit de persuader à la plupart des rois
qu'ils sont le soutient de leur autorité, et ils ont profité avec adresse de
la sottise de l'auteur du *Système de la nature,* qui a bêtement avancé
cette absurdité" (D'Al., V, 409–10).

51. C. Avezac-Lavigne says that d'Alembert "s'était toujours tenu
sur la réserve à l'égard du baron," and frequented Mme Geoffrin's

"Les philosophes ne sont pas bien en cour" (XLVII, 230).[52] Had d'Alembert used the argument he thought would be most effective in winning Voltaire to his view in the matter? However that may be, Voltaire's over-all attitude is well expressed in a letter to his disciple dated 2 November 1770: "Ce livre a rendu tous les philosophes exécrables aux yeux du roi et de toute la cour. . . . L'éditeur de ce fatal ouvrage a perdu la philosophie à jamais dans l'esprit de tous les magistrats et de tous les pères de famille, qui sentent combien l'athéisme peut être dangereux pour la société. J'ignore si les *Questions sur l'Encyclopédie* oseront paraître. Les esprits sont tellement irrités qu'on prendra pour athée quiconque n'aura pas de foi à sainte Geneviève et à saint Janvier" (XLVII, 243).

Voltaire probably knew d'Holbach to be the author of the *Système*. As has been pointed out, even before d'Alembert's visit he had been aware that the baron was responsible for sending the works to the publisher Marc-Michel Rey. D'Alembert would surely have informed Voltaire of the author's name during his stay at Ferney, and his opinion of d'Holbach as a "gâte-métier" would certainly have influ-

---

salon rather than that of d'Holbach. *Diderot et la société du baron d'Holbach* (Paris, 1875), pp. 79–80. In February, 1773, David Hume writes Suard asking him to introduce his friend Mr. Jardaine to d'Alembert, adding: ". . . but as I know that Mr. d'Alembert never goes to our friend Baron d'Holbach's, where my countryman would have access to see the best company, I would farther request, that . . . you would, in my name as well as your own, present him to the Baron." Hume, *Letters*, ed. Greig, II, 275. Inasmuch as d'Alembert, as we have seen, had at one time frequented d'Holbach's salon, it seems safe to assume that the d'Holbach publishing campaign, particularly from 1770 on, had caused the geometer to break this dangerous affiliation.

52. See also XLVII, 124, 230, 243. Pomeau treats in detail the Voltaire-d'Holbach controversy resulting from the publication of the *Système. (La Religion,* pp. 389 ff.). I will touch here only on the details pertinent to my topic.

enced his host's attitude toward that author. In a letter to Grimm dated 2 November 1770 giving his reasons for refuting the *Système*, Voltaire seems to suggest he knows the author without, however, naming him. After decrying the lack of talent in contemporary writers, with the exception of Diderot and d'Alembert, he pursues: "Il y a une distance immense entre les talents et l'esprit philosophique, qui s'est répandu chez toutes les nations. Cet esprit philosophique aurait dû sentir qu'il perdait ses amis, et qu'il les rendait exécrables aux yeux du roi et de toute la cour. Il a fallu faire ce que j'ai fait; et si l'on pesait bien mes paroles, on verrait qu'elles ne doivent déplaire à personne" (XLVII, 241–42).[53] This statement is too open to interpretation to serve as strong evidence that Voltaire has placed Diderot and d'Alembert in a separate category from "l'auteur du *Système*," but the idea suggests itself. In any case, Voltaire henceforth does not openly connect Diderot with the d'Holbach publications as he has done in the past.

A further indication that Voltaire may not have con-

53. Pomeau (ibid., p. 390) mentions a letter from Voltaire to Grimm dated 10 October 1770 as proof that "Voltaire fait allusion à la collaboration de Diderot avec l'auteur du *Système*." The letter reads: "Ce maudit *Système de la nature* a fait un mal irréparable. . . . On a beau dire avec discrétion qu'on ne fait point d'anguilles avec du blé ergoté, qu'il y a une intelligence dans la nature, et que Spinosa en était convaincu; on a beau être de l'avis de Virgile, le monde est rempli de Bavius et de Maevius." A new paragraph states: "Embrassez pour moi, je vous prie, frère Platon [Diderot], quand même il n'admettrait pas l'intelligence, ainsi que Spinosa" (XLVII, 219–20). While Pomeau's conclusion does not do violence to the text, it seems to suggest more than Voltaire actually says. The patriarch may simply have been reminded by his statements against atheism that Diderot's position was similar to the baron's and took the opportunity to send his regards to Diderot whom he had not ceased to admire despite their differences. The subsequent letter of 2 November quoted above appears to make a distinction between "les deux D——" and "l'auteur du *Système de la nature*," permitting a different interpretation.

sidered Diderot responsible for the *Système* is the friendly
tone he uses when speaking of the Encyclopedist. In writing
to Dorat, for example, on 1 October 1770, he states: ". . . les
sentiments dont vous m'honorez, et les vers charmants que
vous avez faits pour M. Diderot, pénètrent mon coeur"; and
he pleads for union among true men of letters, explaining:
"C'est uniquement pour ériger un monument de cette
union que les personnes du plus rare mérite, au nombre des-
quelles vous êtes, ont voulu employer le ciseau de M. Pigalle" (XLVII, 212). It will be recalled that d'Holbach and
Naigeon were conspicuously absent from the group which
decided to erect a statue to Voltaire.[54] D'Alembert must certainly have brought this to his host's attention during his
visit to Ferney, and this would help to explain the latter's
greater severity toward the atheistic coterie following his
disciple's visit, as well as his continued expressions of friendship and regard for Diderot.

There is evidence to indicate that Diderot in fact had dis-
agreed with d'Holbach and Naigeon regarding their unbridled attacks against Voltaire. Despite his impatience with
the latter's position, Diderot was nevertheless sufficiently
just to recognize his party's debt to Voltaire. When in 1772
Naigeon accused Voltaire of being jealous and ungrateful,
and called him a coward or a madman for writing "l'apo-
logie d'un vizir dont les opérations écraseraient les particu-
liers sans soulager l'empire," Diderot came to the defense,
saying:

Mais ce jaloux est un octogénaire qui tint toute sa vie son fouet
levé sur les tyrans, les fanatiques, et les autres grands malfai-

54. This does not seem to have been taken into consideration by
Avezac-Lavigne when he states (p. 192): "Au moment même où Voltaire, par un excès de prudence très blamable, séparait sa cause de
d'Holbach et de ses amis, ceux-ci venaient d'envoyer à Ferney le
sculpteur Pigalle, pour faire le portrait du patriarche."

teurs de ce monde. Mais cet ingrat, constant ami de l'humanité, a quelquefois secouru le malheureux dans sa détresse, et vengé l'innocence opprimée. Mais cet insensé a introduit la philosophie de Locke et de Newton dans sa patrie, attaqué les préjugés les plus révérés sur la scène, prêché la liberté de penser, inspiré l'esprit de tolérance, soutenu le bon gôut expirant, fait plusieurs actions louables, et une multitude d'excellents ouvrages. Son nom est en honneur dans toutes les contrées et durera dans tous les siècles. [AT., XX, 73]

While there is no doubt that Diderot shared the metaphysical and political views of d'Holbach and Naigeon, and may well have helped in their clandestine publications, he disapproved of their violent and often insulting polemics directed against Voltaire and his theism, and on this point there is dissension in the ranks of the materialists. Admitting that the patriarch has thrown himself into the mud in his declining years, Diderot tells Naigeon: " . . . et vous croyez qu'il est bien d'aller lui sauter à deux pieds sur le ventre, et de l'enfoncer dans la fange, jusqu'à ce qu'il disparaisse! Ah! monsieur, ce n'est pas là votre dernier mot." Declaring that Voltaire will someday be great and his detractors very small, Diderot likens him to a work of art which needs only to be cleaned of its surface dust to be held up for admiration, and he concludes: "Bonjour, nous penserons diversement, mais nous ne nous en aimerons pas moins. E facera ogn'uno al suo senno" (AT, XX, 73).

It may have been the knowledge of Diderot's continued respect for him, perhaps made known to him by d'Alembert, that prompted Voltaire to continue seeking a *rapprochement* with the Encyclopedist even while attacking the d'Holbach group. Diderot could well show some indulgence for what he considered a weakness in Voltaire's blind clinging to a deity and his refusal to follow the logical consequences of his own postulates; he was not exempt from the same tendency. Despite his determinism and materialism Diderot clung tenaciously to an emotional idealization of *vertu* exempt from mere self-interest.[55] Thus, whereas d'Holbach and Naigeon were implacable in their enmity toward Voltaire, Diderot retained enough regard for the patriarch to permit the latter to continue hoping for an eventual reconciliation. Such a reconciliation, however, was in fact impossible. Each man's broader ideals and aspirations were too important to permit him to give in to the other. Neither Diderot nor d'Holbach could tolerate Voltaire's apparent willingness to compromise with existing institutions, both religious and political. Scornful of compromise, the materialist party insisted on complete consistency both in their theories and in the consequences such theories imposed. There was no room for deviationists whether on the ideological or the tactical front. Voltaire and d'Alembert, on the other hand, were unconcerned with the individual metaphysical positions of the Philosophes but insisted on at least public adherence to the "party line" in tactical matters so as to present a united front in the pursuit of their objectives. In this way, the Philosophes were always to appear as responsible, loyal, moderate citizens seeking not the destruction of

55. Mornet, in referring to Diderot's preaching of a "morale laïque et humanitaire," states: "On sait que cette morale était parfaitement contradictoire avec son système puisqu'il n'y a pas pour lui de liberté, pas de vice ni de vertu, mais des causes fatales suivies d'effets inévitables. Il a vécu et écrit pourtant sans s'inquiéter de la contradiction; ils s'est partagé entre l'austère enthousiasme du raisonneur pour les froides certitudes des sciences matérialistes et l'enthousiasme fiévreux et même les 'transports' et les 'convulsions' que lui inspiraient les belles âmes et la vertu." *Les Origines*, p. 91. Could it be to force his friend to abandon his Rousseauistic idea of the natural goodness of man that d'Holbach took delight in making Diderot read of the many atrocities he encountered in his historical research? (Roth, III, 212)

existing institutions but the elimination of abuses within the existing framework.

Prior to the civil war within the Philosophe ranks, Voltaire had agreed with his opponents at least in their attacks against Christianity. D'Alembert, however, had consistently argued against a frontal attack and suggested a gradual, evolutionary method for combatting "l'Infâme." The La Barre condemnation, followed by the unbridled attacks of the atheistic faction, forced Voltaire to re-evaluate his methods. René Pomeau (*La Religion*, pp. 372–76), points to the influence of the d'Holbach publications in changing the patriarch's attitude toward Christ from one of scornful derision to one of praise and reverence. Voltaire's final position seems to be one of humanizing Christ and making of him a true deist; thus "le théisme par Christ" becomes his plan (p. 374). In view of Voltaire's previous quarrels with his disciple on the matter, might not this have been another of the ideas suggested to him by d'Alembert? Whether it was or not, it is interesting to note that d'Alembert insisted that Christianity in its origins was a pure deism. Jesus Christ was "une espèce de philosophe" who abhorred persecution and priests and preached "la bienfaisance et la justice." Saint Paul, followed by the Fathers of the Church, and finally the Councils, are to blame for changing this early religion, affirms the geometer, and he concludes in words which could equally have been used by Voltaire: "Je pense donc qu'on rendrait un grand service au genre humain en réduisant le christianisme à son état primitif, en se bornant à prêcher aux peuples un Dieu rémunérateur et vengeur, qui réprouve la superstition, qui déteste l'intolérance, et qui n'exige d'autre culte de la part des hommes, que celui de s'aimer et de se supporter les uns les autres" (D'Al., V, 304–5).

René Pomeau presents the interesting thesis that by building a church in Ferney and preaching a sermon in it, as well as by expressing himself as he did in his article "Catéchisme"

in the *Dictionnaire portafit,* Voltaire was actually attempting to set the model for a deistic church which would gradually eliminate the traditional religion of the nation.[56] This
was precisely d'Alembert's plan. When Frederick rejected
the geometer's suggestion quoted above on the grounds that
the people want an unreasonable cult, the Philosophe proposed a trial for his deistic church: let the monarch build
such a church in Berlin or Potsdam, he asserts, and in a few
years he is certain that the people will come willingly (D'Al.,
V, 308). This coincidence of Voltaire's plan with that of
d'Alembert explains why a reconciliation in the Philosophe
ranks was impossible, for, as René Pomeau states: "La pro-
pagande voltairienne a des visées lointaines toutes différentes de celles d'un d'Holbach. Elle ne fait pas table rase,
elle dresse temple contre temple" (*La Religion,* p. 376).

The task facing Voltaire and d'Alembert following the
publication of the *Système de la nature* was that of repairing
the "irreparable harm to true philosophy" (XLVII, 236)
caused by the d'Holbach faction. It must be shown, first of
all, that the rebel group did not represent the true Philosophes. Of those "têtes légères," Voltaire writes: ". . . il y en
a bien peu qui soient dignes d'être philosophes" (XLVII,
214). He begins an intensive letter-writing campaign against
the *Système* (XLVII, 204, 210, 212, 214, 216, 219, 230, 236,
240, 242, 249, 250, 253, 261, 265), attacking its principles as
dangerous and false, and expressing the abhorrence that
true philosophy has for atheism. To the duc de Richelieu
he asserts concerning his refutation of the work that it was
of the utmost importance that his disapproval be made
known, and he asks his friend to inform the king of the refutation (XLVII, 240). Voltaire pursues the atheists in his
Questions sur l'"Encyclopédie" (1771), *Lettres de Memmius*
(1771), and *Il faut prendre un parti* (1772), even going so far

56. *La Religion,* pp. 430–37.

in the *Questions* as to defend priests (XVIII, 379). It is obvious that Voltaire here is anxious to spare his group from the accusation of being radical, disloyal subversives seeking to destroy Church and State. The Philosophes, as d'Alembert had said, must not alienate princes and priests by persuading them "très mal à propos . . . qu'ils font bourse et cause communes" (L, 355).[57]

The *Questions* is a direct reply to the *Système*. After pointing out that the problem is not to argue metaphysics but to determine whether the concept of an avenging and rewarding God is more useful to society than the materialists' view, Voltaire concludes that his opinion is useful to humanity, and theirs, "funeste." To d'Holbach's accusation that there is only one step from theism to fanaticism Voltaire replies: "Vous craignez 'qu'en adorant Dieu on ne redevienne bientôt superstitieux et fanatique'; mais n'est-il pas à craindre qu'en le niant on ne s'abandonne aux passions les plus atroces et aux crimes les plus affreux?" He then becomes conciliatory and says that he knows his adversaries to be good men and does not begrudge them their personal opinion. It is its practical consequences which he fears: an

57. As late as 1779 d'Alembert was still fighting the effect of d'Holbach's works on Frederick of Prussia. In referring to "le détestable *Système de la nature,*" he insists that "ni ce 'système,' ni aucun de ces mauvais livres, n'est l'ouvrage d'un véritable philosophe, ni même d'un écrivain digne de ce nom" (D'Al., V, 423. See also pp. 346, 348, 351, 409, 421). In 1783, the year of his death, d'Alembert is as vehement as ever on the subject and reveals that he had even wanted to refute the *Système:* "J'ai été aussi affligé qu'indigné de l'incroyable démence et sottise de l'auteur du *Système de la nature,* qui bien loin de montrer les prêtres pour ce qu'ils sont, les véritables, les seuls, les plus redoutables ennemis des princes, les représente au contraire comme appuis et les 'alliés' de la royauté. . . . Si je l'avais osé, j'aurais réfuté par écrit, avec toute la force dont je suis capable, cette bêtise si préjudiciable aux rois et aux philosophes" (D'Al., V, 465).

"athée de cabinet" may be peaceful, but the "prince athée" could become the scourge of humankind (XVIII, 376–80). The d'Holbach faction replied with an insulting brochure by Le Roy, *Réflexions sur la jalousie*, which was attributed to Diderot. Voltaire refused to believe it—"Je l'aime et l'estime trop pour le soupçonner un moment" (XLVII, 79) —and seems to have suspected d'Holbach (XXVIII, 494, n. 1). In his reply to the brochure, Voltaire calls its author an "insensé méchant," gives one of his most scathing denunciations of the *Système* and exclaims: "Je ne doute pas que l'auteur et trois fauteurs de ce livre ne devienne mes implacables ennemis pour avoir dit ma pensée, et je leur déclare que je la dirai tant que je respirerai, sans craindre ni les énergumènes athées ni les énergumènes superstitieux" (XXVIII, 493–94).[58]

Pomeau (*La Religion*, p. 352) suggests of Voltaire after 1770: "Par lassitude, il devient modéré." While there is no doubt that this entered into Voltaire's change of tactics, as will be seen in Chapter VI, a more complete explanation probably is that he was afraid that his own party would be severely condemned along with the atheists and therefore finally accepted d'Alembert's own method of moderation, which the geometer had been preaching consistently throughout his long correspondence with the master. Certainly the La Barre condemnation had been a sobering ex-

58. It seems certain that Voltaire excludes Diderot from the "trois fauteurs" responsible for the *Système* and the later attacks against him. The whole problem of Diderot's rôle in the d'Holbach faction has yet to be studied in detail. Diderot had apparently participated to some degree in their earlier publishing venture. What effect did this anti-Voltaire campaign have on his attitude toward the d'Holbach "manufacture"? Had he by then become, like his erstwhile friend Rousseau, a lone wolf independent of both factions? Perhaps we must await the second volume of Arthur H. Wilson's study on Diderot for the final answer to the enigma.

perience.[59] The authorities' violent reaction against the *Système* again served to illustrate the harmful effect that a bold, frontal attack could have for the Philosophe cause. True, d'Holbach's group had gone beyond the limits desired by the patriarch, but he had taught them their tactics —anonymously published attacks with no holds barred. Now another method must be employed, d'Alembert's. Henceforth the furthering of the cause takes the form of seconding and defending the Philosophes in the Académie française. There are some echoes of the dispute with the d'Holbach faction, as when Helvétius' *De l'homme* is published posthumously in 1773,[60] or when the baron's *Bon Sens* appears in 1775,[61] but generally the quarrel had subsided, and each group had gone its own way.

59. As late as 1774 Voltaire wrote to d'Argental of the La Barre affair: "Cette image affreuse me persécute jour et nuit" (XLIX, 155). And to Condorcet he admits: "Je suis aussi outré, aussi bouleversé de cette exécrable aventure que je le fus le premier jour" (XLIX, 177–78).

60. Calling *De l'homme* "du fatras," Voltaire exclaimed: "Voilà peut-être le plus grand coup porté contre la philosophie" (XLVIII, 399).

61. *Le Bon sens ou Idées naturelles opposées aux idées surnaturelles* had originally appeared as *Le Bon Sens du Curé Meslier* and was, in fact, a corrective to Voltaire's *Le Testament du Curé Meslier* of 1762, which had omitted Meslier's more violent atheistic and antimonarchical ideas to make of him a deist. D'Holbach "rehabilitates" Meslier's memory in his *Bon Sens* by reclaiming him for his party. For an interesting study of the matter see Johann Harr's dissertation, *Jean Meslier und die Beziehungen von Voltaire und Holbach zu ihm* (Hamburg, 1928), 80 pp. Voltaire's reaction to d'Holbach's *Bon Sens* illustrates to what extent he accepted d'Alembert's views by this time. Referring to this "terrible" book, he tells his disciple: "Je ne sais si de tels ouvrages conviennent dans le moment présent, et s'ils ne donneront pas lieu à nos ennemis de dire: Voilà les fruits du nouveau ministère. . . . Votre bon sens, mon cher ami, tire très habilement son épingle du jeu. Vous avez raison de ne jamais vous compromettre" (XLIX, 339–40).

The Aftermath

SIX

THE CAMPAIGN for a subscription to Voltaire's statue had given a strong impetus to d'Alembert's efforts to increase the prestige of "le troupeau." In August, 1770, he had read before the Académie française Frederick's letter praising the patriarch so that it might be placed in their record as a permanent monument "pour vous et pour les lettres" (XLVII, 121). Three months later Voltaire thanks d'Alembert for obtaining a subscription from the king of Denmark (XLVII, 244), and the following month, his disciple discloses his intention to seek a contribution from Louis XV himself (XLVII, 271). Yet this was scant consolation. The publication of the *Système* had made things difficult for the Philosophes, who were being indiscriminately accused of sharing the views of the radical atheists. Voltaire hesitates to publish his *Questions sur l'"Encyclopédie"* for this reason (XLVII, 243), and when he asks d'Alembert if they are in danger (XLVII, 519) his friend replies that things are so bad he is becoming "presque imbécile de découragement et de tristesse" (XLVIII, 40). His election as perpetual secretary of the Académie française notwithstanding, d'Alembert

had had a setback in his efforts to have "right-minded" candidates elected to that body. The king had disapproved of
both Delille and Suard despite their successful election and,
what was worse for Voltaire, his friend the duc de Richelieu
had been involved in causing the rejection. In a despondent
mood he writes his disciple concerning the current persecutions: "Il faut un terrible fonds de philosophie pour être in-
sensible à tout cela," and concludes: "Je reviens toujours
à conclure qu'il faut cultiver son jardin, et que Candide
n'eut raison que sur la fin de sa vie. Pour vous, il me paraît
que vous avez raison dans la force de votre âge" (XLVIII,
133–34).

By December, 1772, things had become even more bleak,
and d'Alembert, speaking of the state of oppression under
which letters and philosophy are groaning, exclaims: "Vous
ne sauriez croire à quelle fureur l'inquisition est portée."
The censors, he explains, cut out from books submitted
to them such words as "Superstition," "Tyrannie," "Tolérance," "Persécution," and even "Saint-Barthélemy; car
soyez sûr qu'on voudrait en faire une de nous tous." An indication of the anti-Philosophe mood of the time may be
had from the topic chosen by the University for the prize in
Latin eloquence. It was intended to read: "What is today
called philosophy is no less the enemy of the king than of
God," but the wording, "Non magis Deo quam regibus in-
festa est . . ." leads d'Alembert to exclaim: "Admirez néan-
moins avec quelle bêtise cette belle question est énoncée! car
ce beau latin, traduit littéralement, veut dire que la philosophie n'est pas plus ennemie de Dieu que des rois, ce qui
signifie, en bon français, qu'elle n'est ennemie ni des uns
ni des autres." What an opening for a good brochure, he
pursues: "Ce serait à vous, mon cher maître, plus qu'à personne, à rendre ce service aux frères persécutés" (XLVIII,
254–55).

The closing sentence has a familiar ring. Certainly

d'Alembert cannot be accused of vacillating in his objectives and methods: the rôle he had early envisaged for Voltaire as the "front man" for the Philosophes is again being suggested here despite the danger of the moment. There is a slight hint in Voltaire's reply that he realizes d'Alembert is choosing the "beau rôle" for himself: "Mon cher et digne soutien de la raison expirante," he begins, "Je pourrais vous dire: Si vous voulez voir un beau tour, faites-le." But he nevertheless acquiesces, saying: "Mais vous êtes nécessaire à la bonne cause, vous êtes dans la fleur de l'âge, vous êtes secrétaire de quarante gens pleins d'esprit; je suis inutile, je suis sur le bord de ma fosse, je n'ai rien à risquer; je serai très volontiers le chat qui tirera les marrons du feu" (XLVIII, 260). Three days later Voltaire announces to his lieutenant that he is working on a *Discours de M. Belleguier* defending the loyalty of the Philosophes to God and king and accusing theologians of fostering regicide. Before d'Alembert can answer, Voltaire again writes his "Bertrand" to reaffirm his decision to be at his service, but he reveals his uneasiness at the thought of the consequences: "Raton tire les marrons pour Bertrand, du meilleur de son coeur; il prie Dieu seulement qu'il n'ait que les pattes de brûlées. Il compte que, vous et M. de Condorcet, vous ferez taire les malins qui pourraient jeter des soupçons sur Raton; cela est sérieux au moins" (XLVIII, 270).[1] But he shows his zeal

1. The mention of Voltaire's letter of Condorcet, who, it will be remembered, accompanied d'Alembert to Ferney, reveals a new phase in the make-up of the Voltairian party. Condorcet, by this time, had become a faithful disciple of d'Alembert who was grooming him as his successor. The extent of Condorcet's zeal for the secretary of the Académie is revealed by Bachaumont who, upon praising the young Philosophe's *Eloge* of d'Alembert on the latter's death, notes: "Cette tournure de l'amitié fait d'autant plus honneur au panégyriste, qu'il essuyait souvent les bourrasques de l'humeur de son maître, surtout durant les derniers mois de sa maladie, lorsqu'il l'accompagnait aux Tuileries et portait le bourrelet pour asseoir moins douloureusement

for his lieutenant by concluding: "Raton embrasse Bertrand de tout son coeur, et lui est bien attaché pour le reste de sa fichue vie" (XLVIII, 271). D'Alembert replies with further suggestions for the brochure, affirming that Voltaire is the only one who can do the job adequately. He then implies that he will do his share in the cause by adding: "Vous voyez bien qu'il est nécessaire que Raton vienne au secours de Bertrand; mais je puis bien vous répondre que Bertrand ne mangera pas les marrons tout seul, et qu'il en laissera même la meilleure part à Raton, pour sa peine de les avoir si bien tirés" (XLVIII, 280).

As was usual with d'Alembert when he had won his master to his views, he sought to show him that he was not standing idly by but was active for the cause in his own way. On 12 January 1773 he tells Voltaire that he is working on his *Histoire de l'Académie française* and that the patriarch will be properly praised in the work. In addition, he reveals that he has proposed that the Académie take up a collection to be sent to the archbishop of Paris "pour les pauvres de l'Hôtel-Dieu" who had been burned out of the building, and he wants to include Voltaire's name on the list of contributors, which will be sent to the king. "Les dévots de l'Académie," he explains, "auraient bien voulu que cette idée ne fût pas venue à un philosophe encyclopédiste et damné comme moi; mais enfin il faudra qu'ils l'avouent, et

---

le Philosophe souffrant; car la vénération de l'illustre élève le portait jusques à lui rendre ce petit service." *Mémoires*, XXV, 290. Voltaire's letters to Condorcet henceforth are frequently intended for d'Alembert as well. On 4 January 1773, for example, he sends "un petit paquet de marrons que Bertrand a commandés à Raton," adding: "Vous êtes obéi sur les autres points." He then announces that he has written a brochure under the name of Belleguier, "selon vos vues" (XLVIII, 266). D'Alembert himself reassures Voltaire of Condorcet's reliability by writing him as follows: "Bertrand-Condorcet demeure rue de Louis-le-Grand. . . . Vous pouvez compter sur son zèle" (XLVIII, 293).

j'ai fait dire à monsieur l'archevêque, en lui envoyant, le lendemain dimanche, les douze cents livres, que c'était moi qui en avais fait la proposition." As it happened, the archbishop was preparing to go to Saint-Roch to participate in a ceremony of receiving "l'argent des philosophes pour les pauvres, dans le temps où il s'habillait pour les exorciser" (XLVIII, 274). A week later d'Alembert announces that the archbishop did not attend the ceremony at Saint-Roch (XLVIII, 281).[2] Voltaire shows his pleasure by writing: ". . . on ne peut se moquer d'un sot avec plus de noblesse. Ce trait, mon cher ami, figurera fort bien dans *l'Histoire de l'Académie*" (XLVIII, 281).

However heartening these details might have seemed to the patriarch, they did not reassure him that it was no longer dangerous to write too openly against their mutual enemies. Indeed, he had only recently been forced by the censors to delete from his latest play, *Les Lois de Minos*, two scenes along with notes "qui feront dresser les cheveux à la tête des honnêtes gens" (XLVIII, 276). D'Alembert himself, after reading the play, had told the master that he feared it may have been a little too hard on "les sots" (XLVIII, 272). *Les Lois de Minos* was an important play for Voltaire ("Je joue gros jeu dans cette partie" [XXXVIII, 287]). First, it was a test case. While attacking "les fanatiques," it was fairly moderate, and the author had warned d'Alembert that if the play failed, "les pattes du chat sont coupées." The brochure on the University's anti-Philosophe subject would not be published, "et la bonne cause ira à tous les diables"

2. On 25 January Voltaire expresses ignorance of this "Fête du *Triomphe de la foi*" and asks for information (XLVIII, 286). D'Alembert replies that it is a ceremony to be celebrated yearly at Saint-Roch. The archbishop's refusal to attend, he adds, kept many spectators from the event: "Le prédicateur, qui est un carme nommé le P. Villars, a clabaudé beaucoup l'après-midi contre les philosophes; mais ses clabauderies ont été 'vox clamantis in deserto' " (XLVIII, 294).

(XLVIII, 260). Three weeks later Voltaire announces that he has had to delete the most piquant parts of his play and thus ruin it in order to make it pass the censors (XLVIII, 286).

The censorship of *Les Lois de Minos* did not cause its author to abandon the party, as he had intimated, but made him fearful enough to write d'Alembert on 25 January 1773 that he hesitated to publish his brochure by the "avocat Belleguier" and would send his disciple a few copies "pour sonder le terrain" (XLVIII,286). The following week d'Alembert, having received the advanced ration of "marrons" and distributed them to the brothers, reassures his master that he is not in danger: "Les pauvres rats d'église pourront être un peu mécontents, mais cette fois-ci ils n'oseront pas trop sortir de leurs trous; il n'y aurait que des coups à gagner pour eux. . . . Bertrand et ses confrères embrassent et remercient Raton-Belleguier de tout leur coeur" (XLVIII, 299).

The unauthorized publication by Valade of *Les Lois de Minos* in a distorted and more daring form was a second reason for Voltaire's special concern for the success of his play. Despite his statement to Marmontel that he was indifferent toward this falsified version (XLVIII, 296), his alarm is evident from his correspondence. "A moi les philosophes!" he writes to Rochefort (XLVIII, 290). "A mon secours les philosophes!" he exclaims to Condorcet (XLVIII, 291). And he asks d'Alembert to unite with his friends to disclaim the pirated play (XLVIII, 295). The reason for his preoccupation with public opinion becomes evident in a letter to the duc de Richelieu. Voltaire had hoped that his *Lois de Minos* would pave the way for his re-entry into Paris: "J'avais fondé sur *Minos* l'espérance de vous faire ma cour à Paris; mon espérance est détruite: c'est la fable du pot au lait" (XLVIII, 292).

A third reason for Voltaire's interest in *Les Lois de Minos* was his desire to win the duc de Richelieu over to the cause of the Philosophes and thus rehabilitate them in his eyes. In his "Epître dédicatoire" to Richelieu with which he prefaced the play, the author appealed to the duc for his support, saying: "Il vous appartient de protéger la véritable philosophie, également éloignée de l'irréligion et du fanatisme." No doubt recalling the maréchal's influence in previous academic elections, Voltaire pleads for his protection of academicians (VII, 170). If we recall d'Alembert's bitterness at having been thwarted in his choice of candidates for the Académie by this same duc de Richelieu, we can imagine his reaction to Voltaire's letter referring him to the above passage in the new publication. The geometer's reply first reveals his displeasure at having his own *Dialogue* inserted in the volume ("c'est mal connaître mes intérêts que de me mettre à côté de vous"), and he turns to the subject of the duke. Although he has not yet read the dedication, he begins, he can guess in advance what the pages referred to say. Recalling Voltaire's earlier suggestion that his forthcoming work on the Académie be dedicated to Richelieu to win him over, d'Alembert asserts that it will never be dedicated to "votre Alcibiade ou à votre Childebrand," and he adds: "Je lui pardonnerais, s'il vous payait ou vous obligeait; mais j'entends dire qu'il ne fait ni l'un ni l'autre" (XLVIII, 341). It was evident that Voltaire had not abandoned the idea of courting the favor of those in power and that his lieutenant was no less adamant in his insistence on furthering the cause "sans flatter ni braver ceux qui ont l'autorité en main."[3] The divergence in policy on this question had never really been resolved between them. Although the personalities had changed (Choiseul was no longer in power), the basic problem remained. To convince his disciple that his courting of Richelieu was necessary Voltaire pointed out

3. D'Avalon, *D'Alembertiana* (Paris, 1813), p. 153.

in his reply a work by Clément and Savetier supposedly containing his writings but interspersing other more dangerous
brochures under the same name. Those rogues find protectors, he complains; to whom can he turn who will protect
him before the king, he asks, and who else can see to it that
his *Lois de Minos* is performed? (XLVIII, 346)

D'Alembert's (and Voltaire's) failure to influence Catherine of Russia to release some Frenchmen she held prisoner
in Poland had soured the geometer still further against the
"soi-disant protecteurs" of the Philosophes and he reiterates his renewed conviction that the only motto acceptable
for "philosophy" is: "Ne t'attends qu'à toi seule." Turning
to Voltaire's reasons for continuing to seek Richelieu's protection, he concedes that he would forgive his master for
cajoling "Childebrand" if the latter were actually useful to
him, but in reality Richelieu is only laughing at him: he is
too vile to raise his voice, in this land of untruth, in favor of
vilified and persecuted genius, concludes d'Alembert
(XLVIII, 361). Before Voltaire can reply, he receives another letter from his disciple informing him that the duke
of Alba in Spain has sent a contribution for the proposed
statue. D'Alembert cannot refrain from again attacking
Richelieu—this time with a weapon calculated to hit a sensi-
tive spot. Richelieu had asked the actor Lekain to give him a
list of twelve tragedies to be played at the court in Fontainebleau. Of the four or five plays by Voltaire, the duke retained only *L'Orphelin de la Chine,* but, pursues d'Alembert almost gleefully, "devinez ce qu'il a mis, à la place de
Rome sauvée et d'*Oreste! Catilina* et *Electre* de Crébillon."
That's what you get for dedicating plays to that "amateur de
lettres," he exults, and he adds sarcastically: "Vous pourrez
au moins lui faire vos remerciements du zèle qu'il témoigne
pour vous servir." To make sure that the patriarch learns his
lesson well d'Alembert expresses surprise that he could be
duped so completely by such a vile man, and he concludes:

"C'est pour l'acquit de ma conscience, et par un effet de mon tendre attachement pour vous, que je crois devoir vous instruire de ce qui vous intéresse, agréable ou fâcheux; car 'interest cognosci malos' " (XLVIII, 274–75).

In his reply, Voltaire first defends himself for having been duped, saying that d'Alembert, in his place, would also have succumbed to Richelieu's expressions of friendship and his promises of protection. As to the passage in the dedication of *Les Lois de Minos,* advice not followed becomes a reproach. It is evident that the blow has hit home, and his disciple's rather satisfied attitude has rubbed salt into the wound. "Bertrand doit employer Raton," he cautions, "mais il ne faut pas qu'il lui morde les doigts," and he adds: "Au bout du compte je suis sensible, et je vous avouerai que la perfidie dont vous m'instruisez m'afflige beaucoup, parce qu'elle tient à des choses que je suis obligé de taire, et qui pèsent sur le cœur." His colony has never been paid for the special diamond-studded watches made for the Dauphin's wedding, he complains, and he could say much more about "ces beaux messieurs de Paris." Voltaire then concludes with another admonition to his disciple: ". . . que Bertrand ne gronde point Raton; que Bertrand au contraire encourage Raton à s'endurcir les pattes sur la cendre chaude; que plusieurs Bertrands et plusieurs Ratons fassent un petit bataillon carré et bien serré et bien uni" (XLVIII, 381–82).

The very next day he writes d'Alembert in an entirely different tone. He has learned, he admits, that everything the latter wrote was not only true but even worse than his disciple had depicted it: there is nothing left to do but to cultivate his garden and d'Alembert's friendship (XLVIII, 383). Since there is no other mention of the subject between Voltaire's first letter to d'Alembert on 19 May 1773 and his changed attitude the following day, it is difficult to tell how he learned of Richelieu's treachery. The effect of this affair on the patriarch seems to have been great, as can be seen

from his concluding words: "Mon cher ami, mon cher philosophe, vous n'aviez pas pu soupçonner le motif de cette
méchanceté; mais vous avez fort bien connu le caractère de
la personne. Vous connaissez aussi celui de son maître: donc
il faut cultiver son jardin et se taire" (XLVIII, 384). The
following month he is still lamenting Richelieu's treachery:
" . . . il m'avait tout promis, et vous savez ce qu'il m'a tenu.
Vous ne savez pas tout, je ne puis dire tout" (XLVIII, 391).
If we recall Voltaire's ardent desire to return to Paris, the
picture becomes clearer. The duc de Richelieu had persuaded him to withdraw his *Lois de Minos* from the theater
which was preparing it, on the promise that he would have
it performed at Fontainebleau for the marriage of the comte
d'Artoise. We have seen that when Lekain presented him
with the list of plays for the event, Richelieu crossed off
Les Lois de Minos along with other plays by Voltaire and
substituted those of Crébillon (XLVIII, 382). Voltaire had
counted on Richelieu to pave the way for his re-entry into
Paris by means of his *Lois de Minos* (XLVIII, 274, 372, 376,
392) and to aid him in obtaining payment for the watches
already mentioned. We can imagine his shock and dismay
over Richelieu's faithlessness; his decision to cultivate his
garden in silence is understandable in this moment of de-
jection.[4]

Voltaire's familiar retreat behind Candide's words in

4. Despite all this, three years later he defends the duke against
d'Alembert's continued ill will, saying: "Mais ce Childebrand a été
vingt ans Adonis; il a été Mars. Je lui ai eu, dans deux occasions de
ma vie, les plus grandes obligations" (XLIX, 580). On Voltaire's return
to Paris in 1778 we find "ces deux vieillards" discussing the assignment of rôles for the patriarch's play *Irène* (Desnoiresterres, *Voltaire
et la société*, VIII, 208). A further study of the relations between Voltaire and the duc de Richelieu would help bring to light the "petits
secrets" which the patriarch said forced him to keep silent about
Richelieu (XLVIII, 397).

times of disgust or pessimism proved warranted by the events of the moment. Just the month before, d'Alembert, alarmed at the rumor that Voltaire was dying, wrote to Frederick of Prussia: "La littérature et la nation feraient en lui une perte immense et irréparable, et d'autant plus cruelle dans les circonstances présentes que notre pauvre littérature est en ce moment livrée plus que jamais aux ours et aux singes. Votre majesté n'a pas d'idée de la détestable inquisition qu'on exerce sur tous les ouvrages" (D'Al., V, 355).[5] D'Alembert's plans for Voltaire are suggested in the foregoing statement. If the Philosophes had to retire to their "jardin," their chief must remain outside and defend them from their enemies. His alarm at the thought of losing so powerful and useful a shield is evident in his letter of 20 April 1773. Declaring how dear and necessary Voltaire is to him, d'Alembert counsels his master to take care of himself: think of the harm he can do to their enemies simply by living and remaining healthy. He is even willing to forget about the duc de Richelieu at this moment: "Dédiez les *Lois de Minos* à qui vous voudrez, et portez-vous bien." And he concludes: "Adieu, mon cher et illustre ami; portez-vous bien, portez-vous bien, portez-vous bien: voilà tout ce que je désire de vous" (XLVIII, 355).

The repressive measures taken against the Philosophes following the appearance of the *Système de la nature* had frightened Voltaire and d'Alembert sufficiently to curtail their polemic activities. Additional factors, such as his failure to influence Catherine of Russia,[6] and the dashing of

5. The following month he reiterates: "Votre majesté n'a pas idée du déchaînement général des hypocrites et des fanatiques contre la malheureuse philosophie. Comme ils voient que leur maison brûle de toutes parts, ils en jettent les poutres enflammées sur les passants" (D'Al., V, 337).

6. See Pomeau's *La Religion,* pp. 347–48, 352.

his hope of returning to Paris via his *Lois de Minos*,[7] contributed to Voltaire's depression. D'Alembert, as was his
custom, sought to withdraw into uncompromising activities to avoid difficulties. When describing to Frederick the
"inquisition" going on in France, he expressed his desire to
concentrate on geometry because "le calcul intégral et la
précession des équinoxes n'ont rien à craindre des chau-
dronniers." His tired head does not permit it, however, so as
a substitute he is writing his history of the Académie française; but when he thinks of the censors, his pen falls from
his hand (D'Al., V, 335–36).

One month earlier, a package sent by Voltaire to d'Alembert had been opened by the postal authorities. "On ne
peut plus ouvrir son cœur à ses amis qu'en tremblant," laments Voltaire. "Les consolations de l'absence nous sont
ôtées: on empoisonne tout" (XLVIII, 346). Whether this
information had anything to do with the dearth of letters
from d'Alembert to his master for a period of nine months
is not known, but neither Voltaire's nor d'Alembert's works
contain any communications between the disciple's letter
of 13 May 1773 informing Voltaire of Richelieu's treachery,
and that dated 12 February 1774. During the same period,
however, there are fourteen letters from the patriarch to

7. On 8 May 1773 he writes d'Alembert: "Vous êtes trop éclairé
pour ne pas voir dans quel esprit on fit *Les Lois de Minos.* . . . Le
détestable Valade, par sa friponnerie, et un autre homme par ses vers
encore plus détestables, ont empêché la promulgation de ces *Lois* sur
le théâtre. . . . Je n'avais pas besoin de ces nouvelles anicroches pour
être fâché de mourir sans vous embrasser. La vie est pleine de misères,
on le sait bien; mais peu de gens savent qu'une des plus grandes est
de mourir loin de ses amis. Je ne reçois aucune des visites qu'on me
fait, mais j'aurais voulu vous en faire une" (XLVIII, 372–73). In a
subsequent letter referring to both Richelieu and Catherine, Voltaire
shows his disappointment by concluding: "Encore une fois, il faut
cultiver son jardin. Ce monde est un chaos d'absurdités et d'horreurs,
j'en ai des preuves" (XLVIII, 397).

d'Alembert.[8] On 14 July 1773 Voltaire complains: "Il n'y a plus de correspondance, plus de confiance, plus de consolation; tout est perdu, nous sommes entre les mains des barbares" (XLVIII, 416). D'Alembert did not remain completely silent during this period, as evidence from Voltaire's letters discloses, but he may have asked the master to destroy his correspondence to avoid having it fall into the wrong hands.[9] In a letter dated 19 November 1773 Voltaire calls his friend "aussi intrépide que circonspect," and approves by adding that his disciple has "grande raison d'être l'un et l'autre" (XLVIII, 502). Three days earlier he had told Condorcet that he and d'Alembert were the true secretaries of the state and of thought, adding: "Vos lettres sont assurément plus instructives et plus agréables que toutes les lettres de cachet" (XLVIII, 502). A letter to d'Alembert dated 1 October 1773 seems to reply to a plea from the geometer for leniency toward atheists: "Il y a de très honnêtes athées, d'accord; mais un Sabatier, ennemi de Dieu et des hommes, ne doit pas être ménagé" (XLVIII, 471).[10] Finally, a letter dated 5 December 1773 refers specifically to "votre lettre," with the comment that Mme Denis and he laughed heartily over it (XLVIII, 511).

8. Mr. Theodore Besterman, Director of the Institut et Musée Voltaire, has informed me that he does not possess any of the missing letters from this period.

9. It will be recalled that as early as 1761 d'Alembert had warned Voltaire not to divulge the contents of his letters "si vous voulez avoir les nouvelles de l'école" (XLI, 261). The geometer was well aware that his mail was being intercepted. In November, 1775, for instance, in a letter to Frederick of Prussia, he adds a note to the postal authorities asking them not to delay delivery of his mail so long, thus depriving him of the consolation of the monarch's letters (D'Al., V, 380).

10. Abbé Sabatier had attacked the Philosophes in his *Dictionnaire de littérature* (see XLVIII, 422, 423). Voltaire answered the attacks in his *Dialogue de Pégase et du Vieillard*. In a footnote he states that while Sabatier pretends to be a "dévot" he actually is an atheist and has written a work on Spinoza's philosophy.

The uncovering of these missing letters from d'Alembert would clarify a number of enigmas. The last cited, particularly, suggests that d'Alembert once again had taken it upon himself to correct his master. Voltaire comments: "Raton avale sans aucune répugnance la pilule que lui présente Bertrand. Ce n'est pas une pilule, c'est une dragée du bon faiseur" (XLVIII, 511).[11] We have seen how d'Alembert, even in times of acute danger for the Philosophes, nevertheless insisted that Voltaire continue writing boldly against their enemies. Was this "pilule" another reprimand for not fulfilling vigorously enough his rôle as defender of the flock? A subsequent letter from Voltaire gives evidence for this interpretation. After noting that Raton has burned his paws to the bone, he begs: "Cher Bertrand, ayez pitié de Raton; vous sentez qu'il est dans une position critique. Il a tant tiré de marrons du feu que les maîtres des marrons, dont il a plus d'une fois gâté le souper, ont juré de l'exterminer à la première occasion. . . . Il faut donc absolument que Raton fasse patte de velours" (XLVIII, 520).

Despite this plea for mercy, we find d'Alembert two months later pressing his friend for a brochure against the return of the Jesuits to France. "Vous allez dire que je fais encore le Bertrand et que j'ai toujours recours à Raton," he

11. Apparently d'Alembert at this time was annoyed at Frederick for having protected the Jesuits in his domain, as well as at Catherine of Russia for having made a flippant reply to his plea for the Frenchmen held captive in Poland. He may have told the patriarch that he would like to write a brochure on both subjects because Voltaire, after expressing amusement because Frederick has declared himself "général des jésuites," adds: "Il faudrait pour lui répondre, que le pape se déclarât huguenot. Je ne désespère pas de voir cette facétie, et celle que vous proposez entre Diderot et Catau" (XLVIII, 512). The suggestion of a brochure making sport of Diderot is intriguing. Despite the constant juxtaposition of the names of Diderot and d'Alembert in eighteenth-century studies, their relations have yet to be investigated thoroughly. I intend to deal with this subject in a subsequent study.

begins, "mais songez donc que Bertrand a les ongles coupés." He then gives detailed suggestions as to what arguments the brochure should contain (XLVIII, 572–73). As in the case of his initial reaction to d'Alembert's *Sur la destruction des jésuites*, Voltaire seems impatient at his disciple's obsession with satisfying his old grudge against the Jesuits and replies: "Vous me proposez de battre un parti de housards, quand il faut combattre des armées entières." But he acquiesces nevertheless and asks his friend to send him further instructions, enclosing at the same time a preliminary draft for his corrections (XLVIII, 574–75). Nine days later he sends to Condorcet his *Lettre d'un ecclésiastique sur le prétendu rétablissement des jésuites dans Paris*, in which he says: "Voici quelques fusées qu'on a tirées au nez de Saint Ignace. Bertrand les avait demandées à Raton. Si vous n'en êtes pas contents, messieurs, allumez-en votre feu" (XLVIII, 581).

Voltaire's pen had not waited exclusively for d'Alembert's requests to be active, however. In spite of his frequent expressions of fear for the consequences of his satires, he had written his *Taureau blanc*, not without some misgivings. On 21 March 1773, he writes d'Alembert: "Raton est très affligé qu'on débite dans Paris un *Taureau* qui pourrait lui écraser ses vieilles pattes et lui donner de terribles coups de cornes. Ces bœufs-là se mettent, depuis quelque temps, à frapper à droite et à gauche; les Ratons ne peuvent plus trouver de trous pour se cacher" (XLVIII, 585). D'Alembert did not share Voltaire's concern but only marvelled at the old man's verve. He tells Frederick that the gaiety in the *Taureau blanc* is inconceivable in an eighty-year-old man and the author of *La Henriade*. "Il faut dire avec Térence: 'Homo homini quid præstat'! (Qu'il y a de distance entre un homme et un autre!)," he concludes (D'Al., V, 349).

D'Alembert was probably convinced that although he and the Philosophes in Paris were in real danger, Voltaire was out of reach of the authorities and had nothing to fear. Thus he ignored his master's lament over the possible effects of his *Taureau blanc* and, instead, pressed his master for another brochure against the agitation for the return of the Jesuits to Paris to staff French schools (XLVIII, 587). The suggestion was lost in the wake of a new development. Apparently, Condorcet had thought Voltaire's *Dialogue de Pégase et du Vieillard* too weak an attack on Sabatier and had decided to publish his own *Lettre d'un théologien à l'abbé Sabatier*. The *Lettre* came at a bad moment for Voltaire. He writes to d'Alembert: "Si vous saviez ce qu'on entreprenait, ce qu'on demandait, ce qu'on était près d'obtenir, vous seriez fâché comme moi qu'on ait fait paraître si mal à propos un si excellent et si funeste ouvrage" (XLIX, 64). Just three days earlier he had written to the Chancellor of France, Maupeou, asking him to protect d'Etallonde, the young man who had been condemned with La Barre in 1761, and requesting that his part in the matter be kept secret (XLIX, 58). The day before writing to Maupeou, Voltaire had told Condorcet that he was about to undertake "une affaire" for the good of the cause (XLIX, 55).[12] Now the latter's "funeste ouvrage" had appeared and was being attributed to Voltaire. What revolted and alarmed the patriarch particularly was the realization that this younger disciple had been tainted by the heretical doctrines of the d'Holbach "église." At the very moment that Voltaire was appealing to the minister and was attempting to engineer, through a cousin in the Parlement, the rehabilitation of those condemned with La Barre (XLIX, 87–88), a pamphlet reflecting republican doctrines was being attributed to him. In an effort to dissuade the public of this false attribution,

12. Two months earlier Voltaire had written d'Alembert: "J'emploie mes derniers jours à faire réformer, si je le puis, la plus détestable injustice que l'ancien parlement ait jamais faite: si j'y réussissais, je mourrais content" (XLIX, 18).

he writes his friends asking them to deny the charge (XLIX, 60, 63, 64, 65).

Voltaire's reprimand of Condorcet for writing the brochure is reminiscent of his attacks against the Holbachic publications a few years earlier. Attributing the *Lettre* to an "abbé," he asserts that the minister will be angered by the statement that princes receive their authority from the people. Sabatier's cause has thus been made one with that of the king and the clergy, he continues: the author of this brochure has furnished additional stones to be thrown against the Philosophes. The patriarch then concludes by insisting that he be cleared of the accusation of authorship being made against him (XLIX, 67). René Pomeau (*La Religion*, p. 352), cites this letter of reproof to Condorcet as evidence that Voltaire has become moderate "par lassitude," but it seems evident that it is not for having attacked their enemies, but for having fallen into d'Holbach's "error" of allying the king with those enemies that Voltaire has rebuked his disciple.[13] Such a blunder was all the more dangerous because the new king, Louis XVI, had only recently named Turgot as a minister, thus renewing Voltaire's hope for an enlightened monarch in France. He expresses his optimism to d'Alembert, excusing the former king by saying he had wanted to do the right thing but went about it in the wrong way, and declaring: "Son successeur semble

13. The fact that Condorcet was the chief disciple of the Voltaire-d'Alembert faction and became its leader following d'Alembert's death underlines the view that, despite the policy of upholding the monarch espoused by Voltaire and d'Alembert, their principles, when unhampered by practical or utilitarian considerations, led necessarily to the same position arrived at earlier by the d'Holbach faction, i.e., church and state were so inextricably interwoven under the Old Régime that one could not be attacked without the other. We can see in Condorcet's *Lettre d'un théologien* the germ of the principles he was later to expound in his *Déclaration des droits de l'homme,* prefacing the 1793 Constitution.

inspiré par Marc-Aurèle: il veut le bien, et il le fait. S'il
continue, il verra son apothéose avant l'âge où les badauds
sont majeurs. Je suis fâché de mourir avant d'avoir vu les
prémices du beau règne dont vous allez jouir" (XLIX, 18).
D'Alembert shared his master's hopes for the future. The
following year he still writes glowingly to Frederick of the
new king, who continues to love the "honnêtes gens" of the
kingdom and has already done away with some abuses.
". . . aussi faisons-nous tous des vœux pour la conservation
de ce jeune prince," he concludes (D'Al., V, 366).

Having set out to rehabilitate d'Etallonde, Voltaire went
about the task with his characteristic vigor and determina-
tion. His aim was not merely a pardon but a declaration of
his innocence (XLIX, 109). As usual, he tried to instill
the same zeal for his cause in his disciple. When he announces the plan to d'Alembert, he complains again of the
Lettre d'un théologien but adds: "Quoique je miaule toujours un peu contre vous, je vous confie une affaire plus
intéressante, et je la mets sous votre protection." The king
of Prussia, he explains, has made d'Etallonde a "sous-lieutenant." Voltaire writes of his intention to tell the king that
d'Alembert is the young man's protector and to ask the
monarch to send a letter testifying to d'Etallonde's good
behavior. D'Alembert is to bring the letter to the minister
of foreign affairs, suggesting it would be good politics to
please Frederick because he may some day be needed
(XLIX, 88–89). Without waiting for an acceptance of the
assignment, Voltaire writes his disciple to announce Frederick's decision to have his minister in Paris intercede for
d'Etallonde, and to warn d'Alembert at the same time to
keep his and Condorcet's part in the affair secret: "C'est à
des philosophes tels que vous deux à détruire l'œuvre infer-
nale du fanatisme, et à venger l'humanité, sans vous compromettre" (XLIX, 115). A subsequent letter asks d'Alembert to use his influence with Frederick to maintain the

monarch's interest in their project (XLIX, 127). D'Alembert, once reassured that the duc de Richelieu was not involved in the plan,[14] espoused Voltaire's cause with enthusiasm, as did Condorcet. Indeed, the latter insisted that rather than limit their activities to d'Etallonde, the entire La Barre trial should be reviewed, a step which the patriarch rejected as being too ambitious (XLIX, 132, 160–61, 177).[15]

Voltaire's correspondence during this period shows the extent of his preoccupation with his project. Almost every letter has some reference to the La Barre case. On 11 December 1774 he sends Condorcet a *Résumé du procès d'Abbéville avec les réponses* (XLIX, 161–65), which he later expands into his *Cri du sang innocent* (XXIX, 375). D'Alembert, for his part, writes to Frederick to maintain the monarch's interest in the affair. On 7 February 1775 he tells his royal friend that Voltaire has just sent him his

14. In an earlier appeal to d'Alembert, Voltaire had admitted that Richelieu had not paid him in five years, but he attributed the negligence to the Maréchal's "grandes affaires," adding: "Cinquante ans d'intimité sont une chose si respectable que je ne crois pas devoir me plaindre." He then expressed the hope that Richelieu and the other debtor nobles "ne me laisseront pas mourir sans me mettre en état d'achever ce que j'ai commencé pour ce jeune homme si malheureux" (XLIX, 115). Voltaire was no doubt referring to his financial straits (d'Etallonde was then living at Ferney), but his disciple apparently interpreted his words to mean that the patriarch had asked Richelieu's protection for the fugitive, and in a letter now lost, must have expressed his displeasure over this. Voltaire replied: "Voyez, mon très cher sage, dans quelle prodigieuse erreur vous êtes tombé! . . . Je vous ai mandé que je devais respecter une ancienne liaison et d'anciens bons offices; mais certainement il n'a jamais été ni dans ma pensée ni au bout de ma plume que j'eusse dessein de me servir de lui dans notre affaire" (XLIX, 155–56).

15. XLIX, 130, note 1, states that "l'honneur d'avoir provoqué la révision du procès de La Barre appartient à Condorcet et que ce fut lui qui poussa à cette démarche Voltaire, qui d'abord, de peur de gâter l'affaire, 'ne voulait pas y paraître.' " See also XLIX, 131, note 2.

play *Dom Pèdre*, which is followed by an *Eloge de la raison*, "une des choses les plus charmantes qu'il ait faites." What a man, he exclaims; he is still interested in "l'atroce et ridicule affaire du jeune homme auquel votre majesté s'intéresse, et qui m'en paraît bien digne par tout ce que M. de Voltaire écrit de son caractère et de son application" (D'Al., V, 358). Voltaire continues to urge his disciple to write to Frederick as he himself is doing, adding: "Je ne démordrai de mon entreprise qu'en mourant" (XLIX, 223).

Feeling a momentary fright for his project when the comte de Tressan attributes to him Cubière's *Epître au comte de Tressan sur ces pestes publiques qu'on appelle philosophes*, the master writes his disciple to express his surprise that Tressan should suspect him of the *Epître*, and to indicate his fear that this error will harm the young man whose cause they are sponsoring (XLIX, 268). After an intensive campaign of denials (XLIX, 272, 279, 286–89, 294–95), Voltaire returned to his main preoccupation and, possibly on the advice of Condorcet (XLIX, 300), decided that rather than ask favors of the Parlement, he would urge Frederick to honor d'Etallonde with a good position. The monarch complied (XLIX, 321), and Voltaire asked d'Alembert to give him "cent coups d'encensoir" which would surely encourage him (XLIX, 339). D'Alembert announced his acquittal of the task and asked: "Etes-vous content de moi? c'est au moins bien sûrement mon intention" (XLIX, 358).

Having satisfied himself by procuring a good position for d'Etallonde, Voltaire turned to other subjects, notably the elections in the Académie,[16] and local matters.[17] The ap-

16. He writes d'Alembert on 8 February 1776, for example: "M Turgot succédera-t-il dans notre Académie à M le duc de Saint-Aignan, qui était, je pense, son beau frère? et si vous ne choisissez pas M Turgot, prendrez-vous M de La Harpe? il nous faut un homme qui ose penser, soit ministre, soit poète tragique" (XLIX, 506–7). The

pearance at this time of d'Holbach's *Bon Sens* served to revive his fears that the enemies of the Philosophes would point to it as an example of the "new ministry" (XLIX, 340). He withdrew again to a protective silence, so much so that when d'Alembert asked his permission to allow Neufchâteau to answer La Beaumelle's commentaries on *La Henriade,* Voltaire refused because he did not want to antagonize Fréron, their publisher: " . . . il ne faut pas attaquer à la fois toutes les puissances." Besides, he adds, he has so often made fun of Fréron that the latter has a right to strike back. However, if Neufchâteau wanted to take it upon himself to defend him "en champ clos" in the *Mercure* or some other journal, Voltaire would be grateful to him for it (XLIX, 364).

In his final years, Voltaire seems to have become more and more fearful of persecution. When he was accused by Tressan of writing Cubière's *Epître,* he begged Condorcet and d'Alembert to help him: "Raton prie instamment MM. Bertrand de détourner de lui un calice si amer; ses vieilles pattes sont assez brûlées. Ils sont conjurés de ne pas faire brûler le reste de son maigre corps. . . il faut qu'il meure en paix" (XLIX, 268). An unauthorized edition of Voltaire's works by Bardin, including some more dangerous works he had not written, gave Voltaire further fears. Expressing the opinion that this "miserable bookdealer" wants to have him burned, he continues: "Je ne plaisante point,

---

following month he writes: "Il faut absolument que M de Condorcet soit des nôtres, sans quoi notre Académie sera un jour aussi méprisée que la Sorbonne" (XLIX, 553).

17. Suggesting his withdrawal from polemic activities when discussing his efforts to "brûler les griffes des fermiers généraux" who were collecting taxes in his domain, the patriarch writes to d'Alembert: "Je ne suis plus l'heureux Raton à qui vous faisiez quelquefois tirer les marrons du feu. Je ne tire que les marrons de mon petit pays de Gex" (XLIX, 506). On 16 March 1776 Voltaire sends his friend a copy of his *Remontrances du pays de Gex* (XLIX, 553).

je sens combien il est dangereux d'être accusé, et combien il est ridicule de se justifier; je sens aussi qu'il serait bien triste, à mon âge de quatre-vingt-deux ans, de chercher une nouvelle patrie comme d'Etallonde. J'aime fort la vérité, mais je n'aime point du tout le martyre" (XLIX, 507). Despite a reassuring letter from Condorcet minimizing the importance of the edition and exhorting him not to allow himself to be so easily upset (XLIX, 513), the patriarch continued to write his friends lamenting his imminent "execution." On 26 February 1776 he writes Condorcet: "L'Eglise des gens de bien est en danger. Soutenez-la sur le penchant du précipice; empêchez que les assassins de la Barre triomphent. Je sais que les scélérats aiguisent leurs poignards contre moi; je sais tout ce qu'ils préparent" (XLIX, 533). To d'Argental he says that they are plotting against him in Paris; he is between the hammer and the anvil and fears he may be forced into exile to die far from consolation (XLIX, 545).

The reason for such terror probably lies in the recalling of the "ancien parlement" by the new king. This was the group which had been responsible for the La Barre execution, and already a more severe censorship had begun to be exercised in Paris. Five months before Voltaire's above-quoted letter, d'Alembert had written to Frederick that the priests and the Parlement appeared to have formed a league against "les lumières," adding: "Ces parlements qui brûlent, sans miséricorde, les œuvres des philosophes, pourraient bien, si on les laissait faire, échauder les philosophes eux-mêmes" (D'Al., V, 367). In this intensified anti-Philosophe campaign, a concerted effort seems to have been made to discredit Turgot and his reform measures. D'Alembert complains of this to the king of Prussia (D'Al., V, 372, 374), and he informs Voltaire that the Parlement had tried to revive the Sorbonne's arguments against interest in order to make Turgot appear as a "fauteur de l'usure." Turgot's enemies in the Parlement were silenced, however, thus avoiding the ridicule such a stand would have brought upon them (XLIX, 594).[18]

Although the Philosophes in Paris were being harassed, Voltaire was really not in danger, as both d'Alembert and Condorcet had assured him. A letter from Suard dated 6 March 1776 seems momentarily to have allayed Voltaire's apprehension. Bardin's edition is not selling, Suard writes, so he need have no fears, and besides, it is not advisable to let "le fanatisme" know of one's trepidation because its representatives are now fearful of being ridiculed. Finally, as if to reassure him of his personal safety, Suard affirms: "Il est vrai que nous somnes dans un moment orageux; 'sed tua navis in alto est'; c'est aux petites barques à se garer de la tempête" (XLIX, 546).[19]

The hope for an enlightened monarchy for France, aroused by the appointment of Turgot to a ministerial post, was soon to be dashed by his expulsion from the government. The reform measures which had so pleased Voltaire —particularly the relief from the tax practices of the "fermiers généraux"—went with him. Disillusioned, Condorcet laments the end of their "beau rêve" and announces his decision to return to geometry and philosophy for con-

18. One bright spot in the picture, from d'Alembert's point of view, was the fall of the duc de Richelieu. He tells Voltaire happily: "Bertrand plaint très sincèrement Raton de se croire obligé de se taire au sujet de Rossinante-Childebrand; pour Bertrand, . . . il ne peut que se réjouir, avec tous les honnêtes Bertrands, de voir Childebrand dans l'opprobe qu'il mérite" (XLIX, 594).

19. One statement by Suard is significant in showing his forebodings of the impending revolution which no doubt the enemies of the Philosophes could also sense: "Le public s'éclaire; il ne lui manque que de connaître sa force pour renverser bien des tyrannies" (XLIX, 546). D'Alembert too shows an uneasiness at the news of the American Revolution for its possible effect on Europe: "J'ai toujours peur que cette tache d'huile ne s'étende et ne nous arrive" (D'Al., V, 372).

solation (L, 29).[20] Voltaire reflects the same disenchantment in his reply: "... je suis de tous les côtés livré aux regrets, et malheureusement je suis sans espérance; c'est le pire de tous les états. C'est même le signal que nous donne la nature pour sortir de ce monde, car quel motif nous y peut retenir quand l'illusion de cette espérance est perdue?" (L, 56)

As if this were not bad enough, d'Alembert, in the meantime, had become despondent over the loss of Mlle de Lespinasse, followed shortly by the death of his friend Mme Geoffrin. Complaining of violent and continual headaches, the effects of his "disposition morale" (D'Al., V, 376), he too reflects the idea that the only solace left him is the hope of dying soon: "Cela n'est pas fort consolant, mais ... c'est un moyen que la nature nous donne de nous détacher de cette vie que nous sommes obligé de quitter" (D'Al., V, 380).

Fortunately for both Philosophes, an event was to distract them from their morbid mood and renew in them a certain amount of enthusiasm. Le Tourneur had just published two volumes of his *Shakespeare traduit de l'anglais* and had dared to call the English author the "God of the theater," holding him up as the only model for playwrights to follow.

20. Voltaire immediately sent Turgot his *Epître à un homme*. It was not the first time he had praised the ex-minister. Mlle de Lespinasse, a close friend of Condorcet and Turgot, and sometimes critical of Voltaire's writings, responded with enthusiasm to the patriarch's praise of the minister's reforms. In a letter to Condorcet concerning a *Diatribe à l'auteur des "Ephémérides"* by the "vieillard de Ferney," she notes that it has "la vigueur, la gaîté et la frivolité de vingt ans," and she continues: "Il y a de fort bonnes choses et quelques traits excellents; ce qu'il dit sur l'édit de M. Turgot est vraiment touchant: 'L'humanité tenait la plume et le roi a signé.'" *Lettres inédites de Mademoiselle de Lespinasse,* ed. Charles Henry (Paris, 1887), p. 155. Concerning the fall of Turgot, Voltaire writes Condorcet: "Je suis dans une amertume continuelle depuis qu'on nous a ôté le protecteur du peuple et celui de ma province. Depuis ce jour fatal, je n'ai suivi aucune affaire ... et j'attends patiemment qu'on nous égorge" (L, 817).

In a letter to d'Argental Voltaire fumes against Le Tourneur for ignoring entirely Corneille and Racine, and he exclaims: "Le sang pétille dans mes vieilles veines en vous
parlant de lui" (L, 56). "A mon secours," he then appeals
to d'Alembert, and he sends his friend a *Lettre à l'Académie
française* (L, 59). D'Alembert, in his official capacity as perpetual secretary, replies that he read the letter to the Académie and its members not only approve it but want to read
it at the public session before the distribution of prizes.
Some revisions must be made, however. The names of the
translators must be omitted, offensive personalities must be
removed, and he must "retouch" some of the more daring
quotations from Shakespeare which might be too offensive
in a public reading (L, 65). Voltaire agrees to the revisions
which he leaves to his disciple's discretion, but he insists
that the appeal to the queen be retained: "Je combats pour
la nation," he explains (L, 68).

The preoccupation with this battle to defend French
good taste seems to have had a salutary effect on d'Alembert
and in a rare outburst of enthusiasm he announces to his
master on 20 August 1776: "Je regarde ce jour comme un
jour de bataille . . . où le sous-lieutenant Bertrand secondera
de ses faibles pattes les griffes du feld-maréchal Raton. . . . Il
faut que Shakespeare ou Racine demeure sur la place. . . .
Adieu, mon cher et illustre ami; je crierai dimanche, en
allant à la charge: Vive Saint-Denis-Voltaire, et meure
Georges-Shakespeare!" (L, 77) The reading proved to be a
great success. D'Alembert is pleased to tell his friend that
not only was it applauded, but the public made him repeat
several passages. It is unfortunate that certain parts had to
be cut out so as not to scandalize pious ears and the ladies
present, he continues, but what he was able to retain caused
a great deal of laughter and contributed to the final victory.
In a somewhat self-satisfied mood, the geometer concludes:
"Adieu mon cher maître; je suis très flatté que vous m'ayez

choisi pour sonner le charge sous vos ordres, et, en vérité,
assez content de la manière dont je m'en suis acquitté" (L,
77–78).[21]

The triumph was somewhat soured by the difficulties encountered in seeking authorization to print the *Lettre à
l'Académie*. D'Alembert tells Voltaire that the "garde des
sceaux" refused permission and that the king refused a request to increase the prize money for the Académie's com-
petitions because the "dévots" of Versailles had persuaded
him that the letter on Shakespeare was injurious to religion
(L, 94).[22] Voltaire blames Le Tourneur for the false charges
and confides that he had planned a second more interesting
letter on the subject but that he will postpone further action
on it for the moment (L, 99–100). A subsequent note from
his disciple informs the patriarch that the ban on printing
the letter has been lifted but that the impression still persists at Versailles that it was "un ouvrage impie" (L, 103).

The impetus given Voltaire by his battle against "Gilles-

21. In criticizing d'Alembert's academic speeches Bachaumont says
their common defect is to have "beaucoup de prétention" (*Mémoires
secrets*, VIII, 241). Discussing the geometer's *Réflexions sur la poésie*,
he affirms that "de mauvaises plaisanteries mêlées de beaucoup
d'amertume, faisaient tout le fond de sa dissertation." But he admits
(I, 133): "Elle a fait rire à gorge déployée." In spite of his criticism,
Bachaumont testifies to the popularity of d'Alembert's speeches when
he reports a meeting which ended "sèchement, M. d'Alembert qui est
en possession d'égayer l'Académie par quelque caricature du jour,
étant encore auprès du Roi de Prusse" (I, 312). On another occasion
he enumerates the items read by d'Alembert in a public session and
notes: "L'orateur, qui sait lire, en a fait passer de bien médiocres. . . .
Quand sa poitrine est fatiguée, il n'a qu'à terminer la phrase où il
s'arrête par une certaine inflexion de voix; aussitôt les auditeurs
émerveillés applaudissent à la ronde, et lui donnent le temps de
reprendre haleine" (V, 357).

22. Similar charges of irreligion were made against Turgot to cause
him to lose favor with the king. See Condorcet's letter to Voltaire
(L, 37–41).

Shakespeare" seems to have revived his polemic spirit and, ignoring d'Alembert's comments, he asks for the name of the author of the *Lettres de quelques juifs* addressed to him, declaring: "Je viendrai à lui quand j'aurai achevé d'étriller Shakespeare" (L, 110). An optimistic note is once more sounded. Despite the fact that "reason and liberty" are not well received in this world, the master nevertheless urges his disciple to hold fast and take courage (L, 111). The pessimistic mood has given way to a renewed zeal for the cause. Perhaps the realization that his "troupeau" in Paris had achieved its desired respectability helped to revive his spirits. La Harpe was now furnishing them with a public voice through his *Journal de politique et de littérature;* Turgot, at least for a time, had had an important post in the government; and d'Alembert, as moving spirit in the Académie française, had made his position as perpetual secretary a sounding board for the party. After the victorious reading of the *Lettre* against Shakespeare, and after reading the highly flattering letters Frederick had written d'Alembert on the death of Mlle de Lespinasse, Voltaire tells his disciple: "En vérité, il n'y a rien au-dessus de la considération dont vous jouissez; c'est là ce que doit faire frémir le fanatisme: il est écrasé sous votre char de triomphe" (L, 132).

For d'Alembert, life had become somewhat more bearable (D'Al., V, 381), and during his "convalescence morale" (D'Al., V, 383), he is even tempted to take up his pen again, but he tells Voltaire: "Je m'abstiens d'être lu, de peur d'être brûlé" (L, 163). Evidently, from his reaction to an anonymous brochure which had been falsely attributed to him, Voltaire, too, still had such fears. D'Alembert testifies to his master's renewed melancholy when he suggests to Frederick that Voltaire's low spirits are due in part to the revival of the Inquisition in Spain, but chiefly to his fears over the brochure *La Bible enfin expliquée, et commentée*

par plusieurs aumôniers de sa majesté le roi de P. The Parlement, he explains, intends to burn the work, which it attributes to Voltaire. The geometer then asks Frederick to de-
clare publicly that his chaplains did indeed write the
brochure, thus relieving the patriarch of this anxiety (D'Al.,
V, 382). Two months later (27 February 1777) he expresses
the sentiment that if things are bad in France at least they
do not have a Spanish Inquisition, and he turns to the subject of his friend at Ferney: "Voltaire n'a point de *vache
blanche,* mais il a toujours grand peur des gens qui font
brûler les vaches. Je le crois cependant un peu tranquillisé
en ce moment sur cette *Bible* expliquée et commentée par
les 'aumôniers' de votre majesté. . . ." A further reason for
which Voltaire is "très affligé," he continues, is that the
watch-manufacturing establishment he has built has become
a burden to him because Turgot is no longer there to protect him, and such noblemen as the duc de Bouillon, the
maréchal de Richelieu, and the duc de Wurtemberg have
not paid him for years (D'Al., V, 384).

    Despite such worries, Voltaire seems in good spirits at this
time. He becomes indignant at an *Essai sur l'antiquité des
Chinois,* by the Jesuit missionary Cibot, attacking the Philosophes in France (L, 149), and he even writes Diderot
about it (L, 150-51). D'Alembert, as usual, encouraged his
master to fight. After recommending abbé Guenée to his
pen, he adds: "Vous ne feriez pas mal aussi de recommander
à votre ami Kien-long . . . le jésuite mandarin qui écrit tant
de sottises" (L, 163). Voltaire replies with an exhortation
not to be discouraged: the number of the elect is small but
indestructible (L, 169). As for the Spanish Inquisition, he
admits he had been wrong in his hopes for Spain and that
it breaks his heart; but he persists in his hope for the future,
saying: "Il faudra bien qu'un jour les honnêtes gens gagnent
leur cause; mais, avant que ce beau jour arrive, que de
dégoûts il faudra essuyer! que de sourdes persécutions, sans

compter les chevaliers de la Barre, dont on fera des auto-da-fé de temps en temps!" (L, 187–88)

It is evident that this final spurt of polemic zeal is not without its pessimistic overtones, and a mild stroke early in 1777 suggests to Voltaire that his final hour is at hand (L, 201, 213). Yet, he continues to interest himself in his flock and asks d'Alembert about Delisle's imprisonment for writing *La Philosophie de la nature*, explaining that someone has sent him the names of the judges (L, 213). A week later, Condorcet informs his master that fear of retaliation from Voltaire's pen is preventing the authorities from punishing Delisle too severely: "Ils ont promis de faire patte de velours si Raton voulait leur garantir les coups de griffe." He has been told by reliable sources, pursues Condorcet, that the best course would be to take advantage of their fears and to maintain a hopeful silence (L, 217). The advice was apparently wise, because three months later d'Alembert tells Frederick that Delisle is free and is residing with Voltaire at Ferney. He explains that the Parlement did not dare back the Jansenist attack against the author for fear of the public outcry; but to save their honor, they did not want to absolve him entirely, so they gave him "une petite réprimande, qu'il méritait un peu à la vérité, pour n'avoir pas fait un meilleur livre" (D'Al., V, 389). This fear of the "cri public" was striking proof that d'Alembert's aim of working through public opinion was indeed efficacious, and the incident faintly presages the enthusiasm which was to burst forth unrestrainedly upon the patriarch's re-entry into Paris shortly afterwards.

Having taken Delisle under his wing at Ferney, Voltaire, as in the case of d'Etallonde, immediately began a campaign to have him honored by a post with the king of Prussia (L, 250, 273, 323, 334). D'Alembert agreed to help, despite his worsening physical condition. He complains to his friend that he is becoming "imbécile, et incapable d'écrire deux mots qui aient le sens commun," and he adds: "Quand je pense à tout ce que vous faites avec vingt-quatre ans de plus que moi, je dis avec Terence: 'Homo homini quid proestat!' Quelle distance entre un homme et un autre!" (L, 313)[23] The following month the geometer informs his master that Frederick has replied in a surly manner that Delisle could go to Holland as there is no place in Prussia for him (L, 337). Voltaire admits that he has received a similar letter from the monarch and suggests that perhaps some Parisian nobleman might need a tutor for his son. He ends his letter with a discussion of candidates for the Académie and expresses the hope of seeing Condorcet as a "confrère" before he dies (L, 338).

The following month (23 March 1778) d'Alembert informs Frederick that Voltaire is actually in Paris, "bien fêté et bien malade" (D'Al., V, 398). The patriarch's decision to return to Paris must have come as a surprise to the geometer. No suggestion of it can be found in their correspondence, and d'Alembert's letter to Frederick concerning Voltaire's death indicates that he knew nothing of his master's intentions until the latter was already on his way to the capital: "Pour moi, sire, quand j'appris qu'il avait formé presque

---

23. We have already seen a similar expression of amazement at Voltaire's energy by Mlle de Lespinasse, who spoke of his vigor and said his brochure had "la gaîté et la frivolité de vingt ans." De Mora, after reading *Les Systèmes* (1772), writes to Condorcet, exclaiming of Voltaire: "En vérité cet homme est un vrai phénix. Le voilà de nouveau poète, comme il était à vingt ans." Lespinasse, *Lettres inéd.*, ed. Henry, p. 267. In connection with d'Alembert's complaints about his physical condition, his correspondence with his friend gives one the impression at times that they are vying with each other as to who is more seriously ill. When the geometer complains about his stomach and bowels, the patriarch replies: "Votre estomac et votre cul, mon cher ami et mon cher philosophe, ne peuvent pas être en pire état que ma tête. Ma petite apoplexie, à l'âge de quatre-vingt-trois ans, vaut bien vos déjections à l'âge de soixante ans" (L, 223).

subitement le dessein de venir à Paris, et qu'il était déjà en route, j'en fus très affligé, ne doutant pas qu'il ne vînt y chercher la persécution et la mort." He was wrong about the first part, he continues, but he was only too right about "les suites funestes et irréparables de ce voyage imprudent et précipité" (D'Al., V, 410).

Not long after his arrival, Voltaire and his disciple had an intimate conversation during which Voltaire asked him what he should do in the event his illness should become more serious. D'Alembert advised him to follow the example of Philosophes who had preceded him, such as Fontenelle and Montesquieu, who had complied with the customary last rites. Voltaire approved, saying: "Je pense de même, car il ne faut pas être jeté à la voierie, comme j'y ai vu jeter la pauvre Le Couvreur." D'Alembert goes on to say that his master, when his illness took a turn for the worse, decided to go through with the plan they had agreed upon and sent for abbé Gaultier (D'Al., V, 401–2).[24] For the moment, however, d'Alembert had not expected such a step to be so imminent. In retrospect, he expresses his amazement at Voltaire's vitality during the early part of his visit to Paris: "Il avait encore à quatre-vingt-quatre ans tout le feu de sa jeunesse." In one of the meetings of the Académie, he adds by way of illustration, Voltaire amazed them all by remembering the original English verses during the abbé Delille's reading of a translation of Pope, although he probably had not read them in thirty years (D'Al., V, 410–11).

Voltaire's verve was not the only thing which pleased and

---

24. For details on Voltaire's confession and burial see Pomeau's "La Confession et la mort de Voltaire d'après des documents inédits," *RHLF*, LV (1955), 299–318. D'Alembert's letter quoted above would strengthen the evidence advanced by Pomeau that Voltaire called for a confessor in order to spare his family burial difficulties but that he secretly repudiated his recantation.

edified d'Alembert on this occasion. The welcome accorded
the old warrior both by the public and by the Académie
had also impressed his disciple. Voltaire had written him a
note on 19 March 1778 saying: "Tout mort que je suis
je compte venir aujourd'hui à l'Académie . . ." (L, 380).
D'Alembert describes the triumphal march to the Académie
as follows: "Au moment où il arriva à l'Académie, il trouva
plus de deux milles personnes dans la cour du Louvre, qui
criaient en battant des mains: 'Vive M. de Voltaire!' l'Académie alla en corps au-devant de lui jusqu'à l'entrée de la
cour, lui donna la place d'honneur, le pria de présider à l'assemblée, le nomma directeur par acclamation, enfin n'ou-
blia rien de tout ce qui pouvait marquer à cette [sic] illustre confrère son attachement et sa vénération" (D'Al., V,
403).

Despite d'Alembert's joy at hearing such acclamations,
he was fearful for the life of his master. A letter from Tronchin, Voltaire's physician, appearing in the *Journal de Paris*
on 20 February 1778, had warned the public that the old
man's strength would soon be spent, and they would be
witnesses to, if not accomplices in, Voltaire's death (L, 370).
Alarmed, d'Alembert had urged his friend to go back to
Ferney to enjoy peacefully the homage he had just received.
But, complains the geometer, his niece, who was bored at
Ferney, dissuaded him, as did several of his friends who
feared that if he returned, "les prêtres" would obtain an
order forcing him to remain in exile (D'Al., V, 410). Tronchin continued to urge his patient to leave for Ferney and
had even arranged a coach for the departure; but Voltaire,
having committed himself as director of the Académie,
wished to remain to fill his three-month term.[25] In addition,
he had assumed the responsibility of starting a new diction-

25. See Desnoiresterres, *Voltaire et la société*, VIII, 365.

ary for the Académie. Tronchin describes its effect as
follows:

La confection de ce dictionnaire a été sa dernière idée domi-
nante, sa dernière passion. Il s'était chargé de la lettre A, et il
avait distribué les vingt-trois autres à vingt-trois académiciens. . . . Ce sont des fainéants, disait-il, accoutumés à croupir
dans l'oisiveté; mais je les ferai bien marcher; et c'était pour les
faire marcher que, dans l'intervalle des deux séances, il a pris
en bonne fortune tant de drogues et a fait toutes les folies qui
ont hâté sa mort, et qui l'ont jeté dans l'état de désespoir et de
démence le plus affreux.[26]

When Voltaire had first assumed this burden he had
promised d'Alembert to work at it ceaselessly, explaining:
"Je veux mourir . . . en vous servant" (L, 380). In his efforts
to serve his friend and the Académie, the patriarch precipi-
tated his own death. D'Alembert writes that he became seriously ill "pour avoir pris dans un moment de travail
plusieurs tasses de café qui augmentèrent la 'strangurie' ou
difficulté d'uriner à laquelle il était sujet." To relieve the
pain he had recourse to drugs but took such an overdose that
"l'opium lui monta à la tête, qui depuis ce moment n'a été
libre que par petits intervalles" (D'Al., V, 404). Tronchin,
when describing Voltaire's obsession with his new academic
duties, notes that when his patient realized that all his
efforts to regain his strength had an opposite effect, "la
mort fut toujours devant ses yeux. Dès ce moment, la rage
s'est emparée de son âme."[27] D'Alembert, who saw his
master "very assiduously" during his illness (D'Al., V, 411),
wrote Tronchin asking him to allay Voltaire's fears over his
condition, explaining: "Je passai hier quelque temps seul

26. Ibid., pp. 365–66.
27. Ibid., p. 366.

avec lui; il me parut fort effrayé non seulement de cet état, mais des suites désagréables pour lui qu'il pouvait entraîner. Vous m'entendez sans doute, mon cher et illustre confrère, et cette disposition morale de notre vieillard a surtout besoin de votre attention et de vos soins."[28]

D'Alembert, for his part, sought to encourage and reassure his old friend as best he could. When, on the eve of the patriarch's death, he expressed "quelques mots d'amitié," the old man seized his disciple's hand and replied: "Vous êtes ma consolation" (D'Al., V, 406). D'Alembert later, describing his reaction, exclaimed: "Son état me fit tant de peine, et il avait tant de difficulté à s'exprimer, même par monosyllabes, que je n'eus pas la force de continuer à voir ce spectacle; l'image de ce grand homme mourant m'affecta si profondément, et m'est restée si vivement dans la tête, qu'elle ne s'en effacera jamais. C'était pour moi l'objet des plus tristes réflexions sur le néant de la vie de la gloire, et sur le malheur de la condition humaine" (D'Al., V, 406).

The powerful effect of Voltaire's presence on the people of Paris, their cheers and acclamations for the return of "l'homme aux Calas," had had a disturbing effect on the authorities. When he had first arrived, there had been a move to cause him difficulties by claiming he had returned without permission, but they wisely decided to allow him to enjoy his glory in peace (D'Al., V, 410). In recounting Voltaire's triumphal entry into the Académie, followed later by the thunderous ovation he received at the Comédie-Française which was presenting his *Irène*,[29] d'Alembert explains to Frederick that this popularity irritated the fa-

28. Ibid., p. 368.
29. D'Alembert describes the enthusiasm at the theater for the patriarch as follows: ". . . les comédiens vinrent dans la loge où il était lui mettre une couronne de lauriers sur la tête, aux acclamations de toute la salle, qui criait: 'bravo!' en battant des pieds et des mains.

natics: "Mais par malheur cette apothéose a irrité des gens plus à craindre que les fanatiques, et qui ont senti que leurs places, leur crédit, leur pouvoir, ne leur vaudraient jamais de la part de la nation un hommage aussi flatteur, qui n'était rendu qu'au génie et à la personne" (D'Al., V, 403-4).

Upon Voltaire's demise, a series of measures were taken to repress the dangerous enthusiasm which his presence had kindled. Describing to the king of Prussia the "suites révoltantes" of Voltaire's death, d'Alembert discloses that journalists have been forbidden not only to praise Voltaire but even to mention his name. Actors were at first forbidden to present any of his plays, he continues, but this ban has since been lifted. "J'en aurais là-dessus trop à dire, s'il n'était plus prudent de garder le silence," he concludes (D'Al., V, 408). In addition, the clergy, besides refusing him burial in the parish where he died, forbade the Académie française to have its customary religious service in honor of a deceased member.

D'Alembert immediately set about to avenge his departed master for these posthumous attacks, and, as he and Voltaire had so frequently done in such circumstances, he turned first to Frederick of Prussia. Expressing his disgust for a country in which genius is treated so shabbily even after death, he tells the monarch that Voltaire had always revered and cherished him and concludes by asking him to give their departed friend the honors which France had refused. Could not Frederick order "quelque acte solennel, qui console la philosophie, qui fasse rougir la France, et qui confonde le fanatisme"? (D'Al., V, 408) In a subsequent letter he becomes more specific and suggests that the Prussian

---

Entre les deux pièces, ils placèrent sur le théâtre le buste de M. de Voltaire, qu'ils avaient couronné de même, et ce fut alors que les transports redoublèrent" (D'Al., V, 403).

king order the Catholic church in Berlin to hold a special service "aux mânes de Voltaire." In the event that they should object, he encloses documents certified by Voltaire's nephew, the abbé Mignot, affirming that his uncle died in the faith and showing from canon law that the refusal of burial in Paris was an injustice (D'Al., V, 426–27). Frederick gladly complies and d'Alembert, overjoyed, thanks the monarch for "le service de Voltaire," assuring him that everyone in Paris, with the exception of the clergy, was enchanted by the news of "cette pieuse et auguste cérémonie. Nous sommes bien sûrs à présent que Voltaire a pour le moins un pied en Paradis" (D'Al., V, 431).

This initial success spurred the Philosophe on to an even more extravagant request, that the king erect in Voltaire's honor, in the same Catholic church at Berlin, a monument representing Voltaire prostrated before the Heavenly Father while trampling fanaticism under foot. This would make an excellent epigram, and Frederick could supervise its execution by the sculptor Tassart (D'Al., V, 431). This time the Prussian ruler refused to comply, and d'Alembert, after urging him to purchase a Houdon bust of the patriarch, expresses his disappointment over the refusal: "J'avoue, sire, que j'ai regret à ce monument, surtout quand je pense qu'il eût retracé aux siècles futurs les honneurs rendus par Auguste à Virgile" (D'Al., V, 434).

D'Alembert did not limit himself to this minor sniping at Voltaire's detractors: he had a more ambitious plan to avenge his master's memory, and his preponderant rôle in the Académie would furnish him the means to implement this project. Although his suggestion that Voltaire's seat in the Académie be left forever vacant was not accepted (D'Al., V, 407), he managed to have a resolution passed forbidding any further religious services in honor of deceased members until Voltaire's memory had been so honored. Further, he

proposed an *Eloge de M. de Voltaire* as the next subject for
the prize in poetry, doubling the prize money from his own
funds.[30] Bachaumont describes d'Alembert's anxieties during his maneuvers in favor of his master:

M. d'Alembert, fort satisfait d'avoir réussi dans les deux coups
fourrés qu'il a portés au Clergé en faveur de Voltaire, commence à convenir qu'il a eu longtemps peur qu'ils ne manquas-
sent: aujourd'hui il se prévaut du silence du Gouvernement et
triomphe. Ces deux coups fourrés sont l'Arrêté de ne point
ordonner le service d'usage pour aucun confrère avant qu'on
eût célébré celui de l'Académicien anathématisé; et l'Eloge
proposé publiquement de cet impie et proposé en vers, afin
d'éviter la formalité des Censeurs de la Faculté de Théologie
qui auraient pu chicaner les candidats. Mais que de peines, que
de délais, que d'anxiétés ne lui a pas coûté ce double projet!
Il a été plus de six semaines à épier le moment favorable.[31]

D'Alembert's success in persuading his academic con-
freres is understandable when we recall his oratorical
prowess. On the occasion of Voltaire's death, his own emotion, added to that of his colleagues, no doubt intensified
the effect of his histrionic talents. Before proposing the
Eloge de Voltaire, for example, he had carefully set the stage
for its acceptance. He had just donated to the Académie a
bust of his deceased master, "le seul que nous ayons encore
dans notre salle d'assemblée" (D'Al., V, 414), and had taken
the occasion to eulogize him during his reading of an *Eloge
de Crébillon.* Bachaumont describes the scene when d'Alembert left the subject of his *Eloge* to speak of Voltaire: "Il
s'est en même temps retourné vers le buste, le mouchoir à
la main et les larmes aux yeux, et l'enthousiasme général
qui s'était déjà manifesté à l'annonce du Prix et toutes les

30. It is interesting to note that Condorcet was to do the same for
d'Alembert upon the latter's death.

31. *Mémoires secrets,* XII, 223–24.

fois qu'on avait nommé M. de Voltaire, a redoublé et tout le
monde a battu des mains, pleuré, sanglotté."[32]

But perhaps the most telling reason for d'Alembert's success in the Académie was his well-organized *cabale* of party
members. It was not mere boasting that had prompted the
geometer to remind his master constantly of his valuable
activity for the cause through the Académie. Frédéric Masson speaks of "l'espèce de dictature qu'il affecta et qui fit du
salon de Mlle de Lespinasse l'obligatoire antichambre de
l'Académie."[33] Referring to the Académie as "sa Compagnie," Bachaumont notes that d'Alembert holds meetings
three times a week following each academic session, at his
home where "l'on met au jour, l'on prépare, l'on combine,
l'on digère toutes les délibérations propres au succès de ses
entreprises; on appelle ces assemblées les 'soirées de M.
d'Alembert.' "[34]

The stereotype of d'Alembert as well intentioned toward
the Philosophe movement but too tepid to be really effective
stems from the differences in policy toward furthering the
cause, as revealed in his correspondence with Voltaire. That
his concern for "le troupeau" was deep and constant has
been amply illustrated in this study. Even the honors he
strove to gain for Voltaire were partially aimed at furthering the Philosophe movement by increasing its prestige
through the reflected glory of its leader. An illustration of
this "party-above-the-man" attitude, even when that man
was Voltaire himself, can be seen in his refusal to join the
patriarch's Masonic lodge as a tribute to his deceased friend.
The "Loge des Neufs Sœurs" had planned to honor "frère
Voltaire" with a funeral service to make up for the one refused him by the church. D'Alembert had gladly consented

32. Ibid., pp. 102–3.
33. *L'Académie française*, p. 44.
34. *Mémoires secrets*, XII, 224.

to make the ceremony more solemn by joining the lodge immediately before. But after a meeting with his "Compagnie"
he decided to withdraw his participation for the good of the
party, because they feared that "cette démarche ne scanda-
lisât, ne réveillât la fureur du Clergé et n'indisposât la
Cour."[35]

Certainly, d'Alembert did his best to impose silence on
Voltaire's enemies by intensifying and augmenting the
honor and praise which he had sought throughout his dis-
cipleship to heap upon his master. It is true that in this
campaign of building up Voltaire as the greatest literary
figure France had ever known, the geometer was seeking
thereby to strengthen the shield and defender of the Philosophe movement; but there can be no question of his real
feelings toward his master. Genuine affection and admiration were mingled with deep appreciation for the numerous
battles which Voltaire had fought for his "troupeau." The
dependence of Voltaire on his disciple, particularly in his
later years, his numerous efforts to please him, and finally,
the frequent expressions of love and admiration he gave his
lieutenant, all help to explain the importance d'Alembert
had acquired in relation to the patriarch's "petite église."
Upon Voltaire's death, the geometer assumed the undis-
puted leadership of the group, and one year later Bachaumont could justly show the completeness of this succession
by referring to d'Alembert as "le patriarche de la secte philosophique."[36]

35. Ibid., p. 199.
36. Ibid., XIV, 296. Grimm, in a biographical notice on d'Alembert,
states that he had become "le chef visible de l'illustre église dont
Voltaire fut le fondateur et le soutien." Corres. litt., XIII, 460.

CONCLUSION

T HE INITIAL acquaintance between Voltaire and d'Alembert in the mundane atmosphere of Paris society was
prevented from developing further by the former's departure for Prussia. Their mutual interest in the nascent Philosophe movement, however, which had just recently found
organization and expression in the *Encyclopédie,* caused
a renewal of a relationship which, this time, was to remain
unbroken until Voltaire's death. The latter's early correspondence with d'Alembert represents simply letters to an
editor of the newly organized *Encyclopédie* showing, in an
exaggeratedly modest style, good will for the enterprise and
its leaders. Those of d'Alembert appear at times to be overly
obsequious, reflecting both the admiration of the little-
known writer in the presence of a literary giant and the desire of an editor to retain his correspondent's support for his
publication. The visit of the Encyclopedist to Geneva marks
a turning point in their relations, and thereafter a more
personal note is struck.

Upon d'Alembert's resignation from the enterprise in
1758, following the difficulties over his *Encyclopédie* article
"Genève," Voltaire showed the extent of his loyalty to the

geometer by withdrawing with him. After this break with what had been until then the chief focal point of the Philosophe movement, a new plan of action had to be found, and it is here that d'Alembert shifts his emphasis from the *Encyclopédie* to Voltaire and that the latter's rôle as the leader of the Philosophes emerges. D'Alembert's suggestions were in no small measure responsible for Voltaire's realization of his mission in life, first, by simply making the patriarch aware of the difficulties encountered by the Encyclopedists and then, in effect, by placing him in the rôle of spiritual director and defender of the Philosophes. Voltaire responded with a vigorous campaign against the enemies of the *Encyclopédie,* and thereafter d'Alembert underlined the patriarch's position of leadership by abandoning the salutation of "mon cher et illustre confrère" for "mon cher et illustre maître."

D'Alembert's appellation notwithstanding, theirs was not entirely a master-disciple relationship. While agreeing on the general aim frequently expressed in their letters by the phrase "écrasez l'Infâme," there were fundamental differences in their plan of attack which continuously plagued their otherwise amicable relationship. The first area of disagreement concerned their attitude toward the nobility. For Voltaire, influential nobles, and ideally, the king himself, were to be won to the Philosophe cause and thereby serve as protectors of the group. D'Alembert rejected this concept and maintained that the Philosophes would have to make their way independently of the ruling classes and achieve a position of honor and prestige through their own literary merits, thus forcing those in power to accept them or appear ridiculous. A second difference in attitude had to do with the method for dealing with their enemies and their respective rôles in the struggle. Voltaire was persuaded of the necessity for sharp attacks made under cover, and he sought to inspire his disciple to emulate his own polemic output, whereas d'Alembert, convinced that enlightenment would come slowly but inevitably, preferred to feign acquiescence to the status quo while pleading for tolerance, and worked unostentatiously to strengthen the Philosophe coterie. He envisaged his own rôle as recruiter and behind-the-scenes protector of party members, leaving their public defense to Voltaire.

The first major clash of these differing opinions occurred over the Palissot play *Les Philosophes modernes* in 1760. Voltaire's reluctance to attack the author because he was protected by nobles, and particularly by the duc de Choiseul, seemed to illustrate the weakness of his method of currying favor with those in power—his enemies had only to do the same to be shielded from his wrath. The displeasure of the Philosophes over his failure to strike out without restraint against their detractor caused Voltaire to be more responsive to d'Alembert's direction and also lost him the support of the Encyclopedic group under Diderot and d'Holbach. An attempt was made to heal the rift by recruiting a new lieutenant, Helvétius, from the latter group, and by campaigning for Diderot's admission to the Académie française; but having failed in both attempts, Voltaire was forced to continue to rely on d'Alembert for the management of his party.

This defeat did not end the struggle over policy between master and disciple. Voltaire redoubled his campaign against "l'Infâme," insisting that d'Alembert take up his pen in the battle. The latter's *Sur la destruction des jésuites* and his promise of more on the subject gave the master a momentary victory; but the consequent difficulties met by d'Alembert dampened his polemic zeal and caused him to be all the more convinced of the wisdom of his original attitude. At this moment, when their divergencies were threatening to become fixed and irreconcilable, an event occurred which shocked Voltaire into a further acceptance of d'Alembert's approach. The condemnation and execution of the chevalier de la Barre, with the ensuing anti-Philosophe campaign, illustrated clearly the impossibility of engaging the Parisian colleagues in the type of campaign insisted upon by Voltaire. Furthermore, the polemic production of the d'Holbach group which was openly and forcefully attacking both church and state seemed to justify the accusation that the Philosophes were enemies not only of religion but of the monarchy. Voltaire could not continue his technique of unyielding defiance without the risk of having his own party branded as traitorous along with the radical atheists.

Armed with these arguments, d'Alembert visited the patriarch in 1770. While little is known of what was said during this meeting, the fact remains that prior to that time Voltaire, despite his disapproval of d'Holbach's *Système de la nature*, was still seeking to avoid open conflict with the atheistic group, whereas after d'Alembert's visit the patriarch's attitude changed and he initiated an intensive campaign against them. Interestingly enough, Diderot was spared in these attacks. Had d'Alembert told his host at Ferney of Diderot's continued good will toward him and of his participation in the plan to erect a statue in his honor notwithstanding d'Holbach's failure to take part?

A further change in Voltaire's position at this time was in his attitude toward Christianity. His earlier hostility was replaced by an effort to transform the existing church in keeping with d'Alembert's technique of presenting Christ as an admirable deist whose doctrines were subsequently falsified. While we can only conjecture, the change in tone of Voltaire's writings and his espousal of d'Alembert's ideas even to that of a gradual, evolutionary approach to the spread of enlightenment suggest that Voltaire was strongly influenced by his disciple. Certainly after this time the relationship between Voltaire and d'Alembert, although nominally still that of master and disciple, changed considerably.

The policy clashes of earlier years are absent from their correspondence: Raton-Voltaire is now at the service of his Bertrand-d'Alembert and looks to him for suggestions and guidance. By the time Voltaire had returned to Paris, d'Alembert, with his well-organized "soirées," had truly assumed the leadership of the party although the name of Voltaire was still used as its shield.

The fact that even after his death he continued to be an ægis for his party suggests that in spite of his apparent capitulation to d'Alembert's views the patriarch had indeed been, and still was, the guiding spirit of the Philosophe movement. Although his objectives and methods at times assumed a quixotic hue because of his enthusiasm and idealism, this very quality made his call all the more forceful and compelling, for his fiery zeal was contagious. D'Alembert early recognized the power of Voltaire's pen and his value as a symbol of the enlightenment and as a natural rallying point for the successful organization of a party. It could be suggested that he abandoned the *Encyclopédie* and sought to build a new party around Voltaire not only in order to avoid personal difficulties, but to play a more dominant rôle —a rôle analogous to that enjoyed by Diderot among the Encyclopedists. This must remain in the realm of conjecture, however, pending further study. Whatever his motives, d'Alembert was instrumental in molding the Voltairian brotherhood into a well organized and disciplined party.

During their policy debates, Voltaire at times showed impatience and even exasperation toward his disciple for his allegedly lukewarm attitude and his refusal to follow his methods. A tendency in eighteenth-century scholarship has been to accept Voltaire's point of view and echo his accusations concerning d'Alembert. Yet there can be no doubt that the geometer's dedication to their cause was as real as that of his master and, if there is exaggeration in his claim that "personne ne la sert aussi bien que moi," he did work consistently in his own way and according to his own concepts to spread the ideals of the enlightenment. He did not work with his master's vigor; but there was only one Voltaire, and every Philosophe, including Diderot, failed to meet his expectations. Yet the real advances that their party made under the guidance of d'Alembert and Voltaire's eventual acceptance of his views suggest that it was fortunate that the disciple refused to abandon his position, for he proved more useful to Voltaire and his cause as an independent agent than he would have had he attempted to be simply a slavish imitator of his master.

SELECTED BIBLIOGRAPHY

Alembert, Jean le Rond d'. *Œuvres de d'Alembert*, ed. Belin. 5 vols. Paris, 1821–22.
———. *Œuvres et correspondance inédites de d'Alembert*, ed. Charles Henry. Paris, 1887.
Avalon, Cousin d'. *D'Alembertiana*. Paris, 1813.
Avezac-Lavigne, C. *Diderot et la société du baron d'Holbach; étude sur le XVIIIe siècle: 1713–1789*. Paris, 1875.

Bachaumont, Louis Petit de. *Mémoires secrets pour servir à l'histoire de la république des lettres en France, depuis MDCCLXII jusqu'à nos jours; ou, Journal d'un observateur.* 36 vols. Londres, 1777–89.
Barbier, Edmond-Jean-François. *Chronique de la Régence et du règne de Louis XV (1718-1763), ou Journal de Barbier.* 8 vols. Paris, 1857.
Boulanger, Nicolas-Antoine. *Recherches sur l'origine du despotisme oriental*. Paris, 1761.
Brunel, Lucien. *Les Philosophes et l'Académie française au dix-huitième siècle*. Paris, 1884.

Carat, D.-J. *Mémoires historiques sur la vie de M. Suard, sur ses écrits et sur le XVIIIe siècle*. 2 vols. Paris, 1820.

Cazes, André. *Grimm et les encyclopédistes*. Paris: Presses universitaires de France, 1933.

Crocker, Lester G. "Voltaire's Struggle for Humanism," in *Studies on Voltaire and the Eighteenth Century*, Vol. IV. Genève: Institut et Musée Voltaire, 1957, pp. 137–69.

Desnoiresterres, Gustave. *Voltaire et la société au XVIIIᵉ siècle*. 8 vols. Paris, 1867–76.

Diderot. *Œuvres complètes de Diderot*, ed. J. Assézat and M. Tourneux. 20 vols. Paris, 1875–79.

———. *Correspondance*, ed. Georges Roth. 6 vols. Paris: Editions de Minuit, 1955——.

———. *Correspondance inédite*, ed. André Babelon. 2 vols. Paris: Gallimard, 1931.

Du Deffand de la Lande, Marie-Anne, marquise. *Correspondance complète de la Marquise du Deffand,* ed. Lescure. 2 vols. Paris, 1865.

Fréron, Elie. *L'Année littéraire*. 202 vols. Amsterdam and Paris, 1754–90.

Galiani, abbé Ferdinando. *Correspondance avec Mme d'Epinay, Mme Necker, Mme Geoffrin, etc.*, ed. Perey and Maugras. 2 vols. Paris, 1881.

Gay, Peter, *Voltaire's Politics: the Poet as Realist*. Princeton: Princeton University Press, 1959.

Grimm, Friedrich Melchior, *et al. Correspondance littéraire, philosophique et critique*, ed. M. Tourneux. 16 vols. Paris, 1877–82.

———. *Mémoires politiques et anecdotiques, inédites, de la cour de France, pendant les règnes de Louis XV et Louis XVI*. 2 vols. Paris, 1830.

Harr, Johann. *Jean Meslier und die Beziehungen von Voltaire und Holbach zu ihm*. Hamburg, 1928.

Havens, George. "Voltaire, Rousseau, and the *Lettre sur la Providence*," *PMLA*, LIX (1944), 109–30.

Holbach, Paul-Henry Thiry d'. *Système de la nature.* 2 vols. Londres, 1770.

Hubert, René. *D'Holbach et ses amis.* Paris: A. Delpeuch, 1928.

Hume, David. *The Letters of David Hume,* ed. Greig. 2 vols. Oxford: Clarendon Press, 1932.

Keim, Albert. *Helvétius: sa vie et son œuvre.* Paris, 1907.

Lespinasse, Julie de. *Lettres de Mlle de Lespinasse,* ed. Isambert. 2 vols. Paris, 1876.

———. *Lettres inédites de Mademoiselle de Lespinasse,* ed. Charles Henry. Paris, 1887.

Mallet du Pan. *Mémoires et correspondance de Mallet du Pan,* ed. Sayous. 2 vols. Paris, 1851.

Masson, Frédéric. *L'Académie française, 1629–1793.* Paris: Librairie Ollendorff, 1912.

Maugras, Gaston. *Querelles de philosophes: Voltaire et J.-J. Rousseau.* Paris, 1886.

Mémoires pour l'histoire des sciences et beaux-arts. 265 vols. Trévoux, 1701–31; Lyon, 1731–33; Paris, 1734–67.

Morellet, abbé. *Mémoires inédites.* 2 vols. Paris, 1821.

Mornet, Daniel. *Les Origines intellectuelles de la révolution française (1715–1787).* Paris: A Colin, 1938.

Naves, Raymond. *Voltaire et l'Encyclopédie.* Paris: Editions des presses modernes, 1938.

Naville, Pierre. *Paul Thiry d'Holbach et la philosophie scientifique au XVIIIᵉ siècle.* Paris: Gallimard, 1943.

Pappas, John N. *Berthier's Journal de Trévoux and the Philosophes.* Studies on Voltaire and the Eighteenth Century, Vol. III. Genève: Institut et Musée Voltaire, 1957.

———. "La Rupture entre Voltaire et les Jésuites," *Lettres Romanes* (Louvain), XIII (1959), 351–70.

———. "Rousseau and d'Alembert," *PMLA,* LXXV (1960), 46–60.

Pomeau, René. *La Religion de Voltaire.* Paris: Librairie Nizet, 1956.

Pomeau, René. "La Confession et la mort de Voltaire d'après des documents inédits," *Revue d'histoire littéraire de la France*, LV, (Juillet-Septembre, 1955), 299–318.

Rousseau, Jean-Jacques. *Correspondance générale*, ed. Dufour and Plan. 20 vols. Paris: A. Colin, 1924–34.

Rowe, Constance. *Voltaire and the State*. New York: Columbia University Press, 1955.

Schilling, Bernard N. *Conservative England and the Case Against Voltaire*. New York: Columbia University Press, 1950.

Sée, Henri. *L'Evolution de la pensée politique en France au XVIIIe siècle*. Paris: M. Giard, 1925.

Topazio, Virgil W. *D'Holbach's Moral Philosophy; Its Background and Development*. Genève: Institut et Musée Voltaire, 1956.

———. "Diderot's Supposed Contribution to d'Holbach's Works," *PMLA*, LXIX (1954), 173–88.

Torrey. Norman L. "Voltaire's Reaction to Diderot," *PMLA*, L (1935), 1107–43.

Vartanian, Aram. "From Deist to Atheist: Diderot's Philosophical Orientation, 1746–1749," *Diderot Studies*, Vol. I, ed. Fellows and Torrey. Syracuse: Syracuse University Press, 1949.

Venturi, Franco. *Jeunesse de Diderot (1713–1753)*. Paris: Albert Skira, 1939.

———. "Postille inedite de Voltaire ad alcune opere di Nicolas-Antoine Boulanger e del baron d'Holbach," *Studi Francesi*, V (Maggio–Agosto, 1958), 231–40.

Voltaire, François Arouet de. *Œuvres complètes*, ed. Moland. 52 vols. Paris: Garnier, 1877–85.

———. *Voltaire's Correspondence*, ed. Theodore Besterman. Genève: Institut et Musée Voltaire, 1953———.

———. *Lettres inédites à son imprimeur Gabriel Cramer*, ed. B. Gagnebin. Genève: Droz, 1952.

Voltaire, François Arouet de. *Lettres inédites aux Tronchin*, ed. B. Gagnebin. 2 vols. Genève and Lille: Droz, 1950.

Wade, Ira. *Voltaire and Mme du Châtelet: an Essay on the Intellectual Activity at Cirey*. Princeton: Princeton University Press, 1941.

———. "The Search for a New Voltaire," *Transactions of the American Philosophical Society*, Vol. XLVIII (1958), Part 4.

Walpole, Horace. *The Letters of Horace Walpole*, ed. Toynbee. 16 vols. Oxford, 1904.

Wartofsky, Max. "Diderot and the Development of Materialist Monism," *Diderot Studies*, Vol. II, ed. Fellows and Torrey. Syracuse: Syracuse University Press, 1952.

Wickwar, W. H. *Baron d'Holbach: a Prelude to the French Revolution*. London: Allen & Unwin, 1935.

Wilson, Arthur M. *Diderot: the Testing Years, 1713–1759*. New York: Oxford University Press, 1957.

INDEX